Center Field on Fire

An Umpire's Life
with Pine Tar Bats, Spitballs,
and Corked Personalities

Dave Phillips
with Rob Rains

TRIUMPH
BOOKS
CHICAGO

Library of Congress Cataloging-in-Publication Data

Phillips, Dave, 1943–
    Center field on fire : an umpire's life with pine tar bats,
    spitballs, and corked personalities / Dave Phillips with
    Rob Rains.
        p. cm.
    Includes index.
    ISBN 1-57243-569-0
        1. Phillips, dave, 1943– 2. baseball umpires—United
    States—Biography. I. Rains, Rob. II. Title.

    GV865.P49A3 2004
    796.357'092—dc22
    [B]

                                                      2003068742

This book is available in quantity at special discounts for your group or organization. For further information, contact:
                Triumph Books
                601 South LaSalle Street
                Suite 500
                Chicago, Illinois 60605
                (312) 939-3330
                Fax (312) 663-3557

Printed in U.S.A.

ISBN 1-57243-569-0

Photos courtesy of Dave Phillips unless indicated otherwise.
Design by Graffolio

*This book is dedicated to my family—
to my mom and dad, Bob and Helen,
for their love and guidance,
and to my wife Sharon
and children Kim, Jill, and Randy,
for their love and support
through all the years.*

Contents

Foreword

Dave Phillips' career touched several baseball eras. When he became a major league umpire at the age of 28 in 1971, he was working games involving players who had been teammates and opponents of Ted Williams and Mickey Mantle. When he retired 32 years later, he was sharing the field with Alex Rodriguez, Ichiro Suzuki, and others who will be stars well into the next decade.

The game of baseball has changed greatly over that span of time, but the definition of a good umpire has not. No one can get them all right, but over thousands and thousands of calls, the best umpires have to be nearly perfect. Dave was. An umpire should never needlessly call attention to himself. Dave never did.

Still, he had a definite personality and presence. He could take charge of a game without being overbearing. During a time when many umpires were becoming increasingly resentful and belligerent, often provoking or prolonging disputes rather than defusing them, Dave managed to be simultaneously authoritative and conciliatory. He earned respect by showing respect. All parties always felt they received a fair hearing. And when a fellow ump found himself nose to nose with a fire-breathing player or manager, it seemed that Dave was always there to calm things down.

Along the way, Dave was involved in countless incidents with many of the game's legendary figures, including Earl Weaver, Whitey Herzog, Sparky Anderson, and Lou Piniella. They all figure in Dave's story. He ejected Gaylord Perry for throwing a spitball, and Joe Niekro for having an emery board in his back pocket while on the mound. He confiscated Albert Belle's bat under suspicion that it was corked, only to learn later that the evidence had been swiped from the umpires' locker room.

Then there was Disco Demolition Night at Comiskey Park in 1979. Few would dispute that Bill Veeck's intentions were noble, but his promotional brainstorm—blowing up disco records brought to the stadium by fans—went more than slightly awry. A fire ignited in center field, and the ensuing conflagration forced the Chisox to forfeit the second game of a doubleheader to Detroit. (Even more regrettably, a few copies of "Boogie Fever" somehow remain in circulation.)

Dave also recalls here the infamous episode during the 1985 American League Championship Series between Kansas City and Toronto, when a close call went against the hometown Blue Jays. Fans in the outfield showered Dave with coins and debris. Upstairs in the broadcast booth, Tony Kubek and I had the advantage of watching replays from numerous angles, and we still couldn't tell for sure whether Lloyd Moseby, the Toronto center fielder, had caught or trapped the ball in shallow center. I told Dave later that plays like that increased my appreciation of just how difficult and pressure-filled a job it is to be a major league umpire.

Dave was among the very best in his demanding profession, but he always believed the players should be the stars, and that the best thing that could be said about an umpire was that he had gone almost unnoticed—because that usually meant he had done a good job. He took that job very seriously, and honestly felt privileged to do it.

His love for the game showed every day, not only among his peers, but also with the players and managers with whom he shared the field. Dave was always enthusiastic, always upbeat, always accessible and helpful to writers and broadcasters, and always genuinely concerned with the best interests of the game of baseball.

This is the story of a first-rate baseball citizen. If everyone who considers Dave Phillips a friend buys this book, that alone should make it a best seller.

—Bob Costas
NBC and HBO Sports

Acknowledgments

I would like to thank several people who not only helped make this book a reality, but who were also instrumental in helping me reach the majors and achieve a long and enjoyable career.

I have to thank all of the umpiring partners I was fortunate to work with over the years, especially Larry Barnett, Jim Evans, Dale Scott, Rocky Roe, Bill Haller, Steve Palermo, Frannie Walsh, and the late Durwood Merrill. Thanks to Dick Butler for believing in me and giving me the opportunity to work in the major leagues.

Bob Costas has been a longtime friend, and I thank him for taking the time and effort to write the Foreword for this book.

Bob Broeg, a former sports editor and columnist with the *St. Louis Post-Dispatch,* has been a great friend over the years and I thank him for all of the help he has provided.

I would also like to thank my family—my wife of 39 years, Sharon, and our children, Kim Groneck, Jill Collier, and Randy. Kim read through the drafts of the manuscript and made numerous suggestions, for which I am grateful.

This book would not have been possible without the work of Rob Rains, and he has my deepest appreciation. Thanks also to our editor at Triumph Books, Blythe Hurley, and to Mitch Rogatz and Tom Bast for believing my stories were worth sharing with you, the reader.

I hope everyone enjoys the book.

1

An Umpire's Life

There is a popular belief among baseball fans that being a major league umpire is a pretty good job. Fans see umpires work about three hours a day and notice how they travel first class all over the country, watch some of the greatest athletes in the world from very close by, and receive five months of vacation in the winter. Someone once said umpires have "the best seat in the house, but you have to stand," and I can't disagree with that.

As someone who spent 32 years umpiring in the major leagues, I admit that sounds like a pretty good job description. But there is much more involved in being an umpire than fans—and many times even those people who work inside the game—understand or appreciate. Umpires are sometimes taken for granted, although I have always felt the six-week strike in 1979 went a long way toward giving us the credibility and respect that we deserve. We had earned that credibility, and the men hired to replace us didn't have it. People found out not just anybody can do this job.

Fans watching from the stands see the basic calls an umpire has to make—safe or out, fair or foul, ball or strike—and they think it is an easy job. They don't see the intangible skills an umpire has to possess to be successful, and they don't see the sacrifices an umpire has to make in regard to his family and personal life.

Is it a great job? In the major leagues, the answer is yes. But it wasn't always that way before Richie Phillips and others improved the pay scale and working conditions. On the other hand, many umpires work in the minor leagues for years, for less than glamorous pay in less than ideal working conditions, but never get rewarded with the welcome news that they have been promoted to the majors. For them, the answer unfortunately is no, it's not a great job.

Is it a fun job? That depends largely on the other three gentlemen you happen to be assigned to work with in a particular year. I was on crews where I laughed so much that tears rolled down my face. Having partners like Rocky Roe, Dale Scott, Durwood Merrill, Ron Luciano, Bill Haller, Larry Barnett, Jim Evans, Tim McClelland, Jim Joyce, and Steve Palermo would make anyone laugh and enjoy the job. You couldn't have very many bad days hanging around those kinds of men. Also, getting to know a lot of other great umpires, even if I didn't work with them that often or on a regular basis, made the job fun—people like Ed Montague, Randy Marsh, Don Denkinger, Ted Hendry, Larry McCoy, John Kibler, Rich Garcia, and Terry Tata. I was also fortunate enough to work four World Series, and three of them were with Lee Weyer, a treat in itself. He was an absolutely super guy, who had fun, made the job fun, and was a good umpire.

Is it an easy job? No. There are many more physical requirements than people realize, and the stress level might be among the highest for any profession in the country. If you had asked Don Denkinger after the 1985 World Series if being an umpire was an easy job, you might not have wanted to wait for his reply. I always hoped that when I was introduced to strangers no one would mention that I was an umpire—I thought there was a remote chance they would like me if they didn't know.

Nobody likes umpires until they get to know them. By the basic definition of the job, you are making calls that one team and thousands of fans are going to disagree with. The ability to make difficult calls and not have people constantly upset with you is one of the intangibles necessary to be a good and effective umpire. You have to know how to handle people and control situations.

I became an umpire when I was 14 years old for one simple reason: money. I was playing on a pretty good team, and the local YMCA in St. Louis was having trouble getting umpires. A representative came and talked to our team to see if anybody was interested. Nobody raised his hand until he said the job paid $5 a game; then 14 hands went up. A few years later, I was told by a scout that I ought to consider becoming a professional umpire. I decided to quit college and go to umpire's school. My father was totally opposed to it, even though he had been a minor league umpire for many years, reaching the Triple A level. My dad, like most fathers, wanted his son to have more success than he had, but he also wanted to prevent his son from experiencing the heartache he felt when he didn't reach his goal. Many people have told me over the years that my dad, Bob Phillips, was a very good umpire and should have worked in the major leagues, but he never got that opportunity.

The morning I left St. Louis to drive to the umpire's school in Florida in January 1964, I was already becoming homesick and was tearing up before I crossed the Eads Bridge over the Mississippi River into Illinois. I made it to the school in Florida, pulled up in front of the building, and couldn't force myself to get out of the car. I seriously considered pulling out of the parking lot and heading directly back to St. Louis, before I finally worked up enough courage to get out of the car and walk inside the building. What I found out was that everybody there had the same insecurity I had: fear of the unknown.

Did I know exactly what I was getting into? Of course not. Even with the knowledge obtained at the elbow of my father, I had no idea what direction my career and life would take. One of my dearest friends in the world, and a fellow major league umpire for 29 years whom I met in umpire's school, Larry Barnett, was my partner for a year in the Class A Midwest League. As we drove all over Iowa, Illinois, and Wisconsin, we speculated about our futures. We had no idea if we would make it to the majors, how long we would be there, or how much money we would make. We were making $315 a month and seven cents a mile expense money. The salary of a major league umpire was so far off in the distance we could only dream about it. But I think those lean, uncertain times helped build my character. You can appreciate success more when you know how hard you had to work to get there.

There is no question I would not have been a major league umpire for as long as I was without a loving and supportive family. My parents, Bob and Helen, knew about the lifestyle, and they knew what it would take for me to be successful. Once I made the decision to become an umpire, they were extremely supportive. My father was always my biggest booster. He taught me what it meant to be an umpire. I had the privilege of being in the locker room with him when he was umpiring, and I watched and listened. I sensed the loyalty all umpires had for one another long before I knew this was what I wanted to do with my life.

I have often said the proudest moment of my career was working the 1982 World Series in my hometown of St. Louis, with my father in the stands. He died suddenly a few months later, and the fact that we were able to share and enjoy that Series will never be matched.

My brother, Greg, was also extremely supportive. He is six years younger than I am and was raised in a different atmosphere, the sixties, when the antiestablishment movement and the war in Vietnam put a lot of pressure on young adults. When Greg was 13 years old, he wrote a poem about his big brother the umpire, which I still have.

Growing up in the fifties, life was much simpler than it was a decade later, and certainly was much simpler than it is today. I remember running the mile home from grade school in October in hopes I would get there in time to watch the last few innings of the World Series games on our black-and-white television set with my dad. In those lazy days, my friends and I could go out and play all day in the summer, and our parents didn't know or care where we were, as long as we were home before dark. Now, if a kid is gone for a couple of hours and his parents don't know where he is, they think he's been kidnapped.

We played baseball every day. I played by myself also, throwing the ball against the front steps and then trying to catch it. If the ball hit the step just the right way and rebounded a long way, suddenly Stan Musial, my hero, was the batter.

I was fortunate to marry my high school sweetheart, Sharon, and together we raised three wonderful children. She did all of the hard work because I was gone so much, and she is a great wife and a wonderful mother. Our two daughters, Kim and Jill, both have their master's degrees and now have children of their own. Our son, Randy, is about to graduate from the University of Kansas and take his place in the workforce.

Sharon's parents, Harry and Lois, and her sister, Doris, also were very supportive of me and my career.

Being gone so much, I missed several special moments in their lives: first communions, baptisms, reunions. Jill was the queen of her senior prom in high school, and I wasn't there to see her walk down the aisle. Kim was a cheerleader, and I missed going to her games. That is why so many umpires don't want to work the All-Star Game or postseason games, so they can be home and be there for some of the special moments in their families' lives, like watching their sons quarterback the high school football team. In my case, Randy was on the high school golf team, and I was not able to watch his matches.

Bob Burnes was the longtime sports editor of the *St. Louis Globe-Democrat,* and he wrote a column in 1964 about umpires. It was headlined "What It Means to Be an Umpire." He was writing specifically in support of the National League umpires' attempts to secure a pension, but many of the points that he made are still incredibly accurate 40 years later. Many things about the job have not changed in all those years.

"You are a lucky guy, you are," Burnes wrote. "That's what people tell you. See the world. Work a couple of hours a night. What a life.

"But you are never home. A player moans about his schedule but he enjoys home cooking 81 out of the 162 days. Every town is a strange town to an umpire. . . . It has its compensations. Ninety percent of the players like you personally. You respond in the same proportion. They'll rage at you, which is normal. It rolls away the minute the incident is over. Only a few carry grudges.

"You like to laugh. You have a million good stories with which you regale off-season audiences."

I was fortunate to make it home for the birth of all three of my children. I was working in the Midwest League in Burlington, Iowa, when I got an early-morning phone call that Sharon was going to the hospital to deliver Kim. Larry Barnett got me closer to St. Louis in our car, and then we met my father. He got me to the hospital in time. Larry drove back to Burlington to work the last game.

When Jill was born, I had just returned home from the International League. Even though I was home, I still thought I was going to miss her birth. After taking Sharon to the hospital, I was told to go home and sleep because it would be several hours before the baby would be born. The nurses said they would call in plenty of time for me to get back to the hospital.

When the telephone call came, I naturally was in a hurry. I rushed out to start the car, and there was a loud noise and a squeal I had never heard before. I got out and immediately raised the hood. There was Kim's cat, Mittens, staring up at me, strangled to death in the fan belt as I tried to start the car. The cat apparently had crawled up in the engine to try to stay warm on that cool September morning. I called my father, and luckily, he was home and able to get me to the hospital in time for Jill's arrival.

After spending all day at the hospital, I was ready to go home. I went out to the parking lot and tried to remember where I had parked the car—and then I remembered the Mittens fiasco. I took a cab home, and several days later finally worked up the nerve to tell my five-year-old daughter what had happened to her pet. Thirty-three years later, I still feel bad about it.

An umpire really has two families: the one at home and the men he works with every day. You share as much or more time with them as you do your wife and children, and you become very close. I tried to fly home during the season as often as possible, even if I could only be there for 12 or 15 hours, because it shortened the week and the season for me. The families of many of the umpires used to go to spring training together, and the kids got to know each other, and the wives all became close. It really became an extended family.

There is a feeling among some baseball fans that umpires don't care about what happens in the game. Nothing could be further from the truth. We care deeply about what happens. When an umpire makes a bad call, it stays with him for a long time. When you work a perfect game, nobody notices you, and that's just the way you like it. I don't know how many thousands of calls I made in my career, but the only ones I truly remember are the ones I missed.

Having a good time while we were working helped make the job pleasant. Many umpires were big practical jokers when I came to the big leagues. In the days before cell phones, John Rice and others bought toy phones that rang. They would set them off on planes, getting weird stares from the other passengers. One time Rice took a phone out to home plate, made it ring, and told Tigers manager Mayo Smith that the call was for him. Mayo actually picked up the phone and said hello, while everybody else was doubled over laughing.

Those moments are gone from the game now. It has become far too serious. You no longer can tell rookies to go find the key to the batter's box, or bring you a left-handed bat. Money has changed the game. It was a different game when I broke into the majors, and I think it was a better game. It was more fun.

One of the highlights of my career has been the people I was able to meet and consider friends, not just my fellow umpires but players, managers, and other baseball officials as well. My career might have ended in the minors if Dick Butler, the supervisor of umpires in the American League, had not taken a liking to me, and I am eternally grateful to him.

Several players stand out: people like Rod Carew, George Brett, Carl Yastrzemski, Robin Yount, Paul Molitor, Tony Oliva, Kirby Puckett, Cal Ripken, Frank Robinson, Brooks Robinson, Al Kaline, Alex Rodriguez, Ken Griffey Jr., and Ivan Rodriguez. I think Reggie Jackson was the greatest clutch hitter I ever saw.

Richie Allen was portrayed as a miserable person by the media, but I always thought he was a great guy. He and Ted Williams, when he was managing the Senators, would come into the umpires' dressing room to get away from the press, and we had wonderful conversations. Richie was one of the best hitters I ever saw.

I saw pitchers such as Roger Clemens, Nolan Ryan, Steve Carlton, Pedro Martinez, Ron Guidry, Catfish Hunter, Ferguson Jenkins, Vida Blue, Don Sutton, Gaylord Perry, Bert Blyleven, and Randy Johnson. The best home-run hitters I ever saw were Mark McGwire, Allen, Griffey, Frank Howard, Cecil Fielder, and Barry Bonds, although the longest home run I ever saw was hit by Jose Canseco, during the playoffs in Toronto, into the fifth deck at the SkyDome. The best defensive player was Brooks Robinson, but the single best catch I ever saw was in Kansas City, when Jim Edmonds of the Angels made a miraculous backward diving catch in center field.

For managers, I don't think anybody was better than Billy Martin, at least for the first two years with a team, no matter what team he was with. He always seemed to self-destruct after that, but for those first two years, he was terrific. I loved Chuck Tanner, and I had more than my share of moments with Earl Weaver. I always respected and enjoyed Tony LaRussa and Sparky Anderson. Another who stands out is Bobby Cox, now with Atlanta. He is a baseball man from days gone by. I first met him when I was playing in the Texas League. He is definitely a throwback. A lot of his knowledge about managing came from Ralph Houk, and the biggest skill he learned was how to be detailed about every player's role on the team. He's not a rah-rah, buddy-buddy kind of guy, but he is a true professional—although he gets ejected quite often now.

Bobby was the only player in my entire career who could call a pitch and bat at the same time. He always said "nope" if he wasn't going to swing at it and thought it was a ball. Most of the time he was right, but on occasion I would have to say "yep" if it was a strike. I am happy for the success he has had.

Other managers, coaches, and baseball officials I admired over the years included people like Joe Torre, Tom Kelly, Don Zimmer, Jimy Williams, Jim Leyland, Dick Howser, Whitey Herzog, Joe Nossek, Jerry Manuel, Jim Fregosi, Doug Radar, Tom Trebelhorn, Sam Perlozzo, Jack McKeon, Jeff Torborg, Dave McKay, John McNamara, John McLaren, Arthur Richman, Walt Jocketty, Ernie Harwell, and the Lachemann brothers, Rene and Marcel.

I would also like to make a special mention of John Hirschbeck, Tim Welke, and Joe Brinkman, whose efforts went a long way toward forming the new umpires union.

Umpires are a lot like players and managers when they begin their careers. They hope to be major leaguers, and they know it takes luck as well as skill to get there. As Barnett and I would speculate about our careers, I often thought if I could just get to the Triple A level, as my father had, I could use that as a springboard to another career. As it turned out, both Larry and I far exceeded our expectations.

I never thought I would umpire in the major leagues for 32 years. I never thought I would work four World Series, plus numerous playoff series and All-Star Games. I never thought I would go to Japan because of baseball, or to Europe to speak at baseball clinics. I was truly fortunate to find something that I loved to do and turn it into a great career.

Somebody once told me that so many things happened to me during my career, I could write a book. He was right.

2
The Minors

My father was an umpire in the minor leagues for many years, and he often spoke about the negative aspects of the job. Even though he loved umpiring, he wanted to make certain I knew how hard the job was going to be. I was a typical kid: "Yeah, yeah, but I'm going to make it." Of course, I decided to become an umpire only when I realized I was not going to become the next Stan Musial. I was like every other kid in the fifties. I wanted to hit home runs, make diving catches, and have fans screaming for me—not *at* me.

I will admit that sitting in my car outside the Cincinnati Reds' minor league complex in March 1964, I had serious doubts about beginning my chosen career. I sat there for about 10 minutes working up enough courage to walk in the front door. It was the same battle I'd had with myself three months earlier when I arrived in Florida to attend umpiring school. Did I really want to do this?

When I entered the complex, a gentleman was sitting behind the desk. It turned out he was Herk Robinson, who at the time was the Reds' assistant farm director and later became the general manager of the Royals. He looked up and started barking at me: "You know the players are supposed to come in through the back door. Don't come in the front office."

I walked over to him, feeling very timid, and said, "Sir, I'm not one of the players. I'm an umpire."

So he did what most people do when talking to an umpire—he began screaming at me. "Where have you been?"

I tried to tell him I had received my spring-training assignment late, but he wasn't interested. He told me to go to the locker room and get ready to work a game that day.

I asked where the umpires' dressing room was located, and he just shook his head and explained there was no separate dressing room. I asked who the other umpire was, and again he shook his head—I was the only umpire they had.

The only locker that was not being used by a player was next to the door. I again was questioning why I was there. I was giving serious thought to getting in my new 1964 Pontiac four-speed and driving back to St. Louis, ending my career the same day it began.

As I was getting dressed for the game, I heard spikes striking the concrete floor. The shoes stopped right in front of me. I looked up, and an old, bald-headed man was staring down at me. He said, "What are you going to do?" I had all my gear on, and it was obvious I was going to umpire. He laughed. "Kid, they will eat you alive," he said. Then he turned and walked out the door, laughing. I thought I had been nervous before; now I was petrified.

As he walked away, I saw the name on the back of his jersey: Cassini. As in Jack Cassini. I never forgot it. Years later, after I had been in the major leagues for many years, I was working first base at a game in Cleveland. The Indians had made some coaching changes, and when a new coach came out to first base and started talking to me, I noticed the name on the back of his jersey: Cassini. He had spent all of that time in the minors before coming to the majors. I had often thought if I saw him again, I would bury him, telling him that story and that I was the kid umpire he had tried to intimidate. Out of courtesy and compassion for a lifelong minor leaguer, however, I never did—but I would have loved to.

After my first game, the Reds told me to report to the Floridian Hotel. When I checked in, the clerk said, "Yes, you will be rooming with Jose Valenti. I think he's with the Macon ballclub." I just stood there. "Miss, I'm an umpire. I cannot stay with one of the players," I said.

Very aggravated, she checked all of the rooms and finally said sarcastically, "Would a trainer be OK to stay with you?" (Apparently she did not care for umpires either.) I said that would be great. It was the best thing that happened to me that spring. He was an older gentleman named Doc Cole, and he really mentored me. He no doubt realized I was in desperate need of a friend.

Umpires were expected to eat meals with the players at what they called a training table. I tried to go there when most of the players were out. I was always by myself and didn't enjoy players yelling at me in the dining room as well as on the field. I would save my money and go to Morrison's Cafeteria as often as I could. One night when I was eating out, I heard there was an outbreak of diarrhea among people who had eaten at the training table. I almost wished I had been there because almost everybody who ate there got the next day off.

My first problem as a professional umpire was with a batter named Jack Hutchinson. He was the son of Fred Hutchinson, the manager of the Reds at that time, and was playing in their farm system. I ejected him for calling me a name, but he said he wasn't going to leave. I really didn't know what I was going to do. Luckily, a manager, Red Davis, a longtime Reds coach and instructor, yelled at Hutchinson. "He ejected you. Get going. Start running and don't stop until I tell you to stop." That must have been the fine for spring-training ejections—running.

I've always remembered Red for that, because I don't know what I would have done if he had not stepped in and gotten Hutchinson to leave. That kind of situation had never come up during my games at the YMCA.

One of the friends I had made during umpiring school, Larry Barnett, had been assigned to the Red Sox camp in Winter Haven, and he called me one night to see how my spring was going. I complained about how hard I was working—umpiring two games a day, by myself—and then I asked about his spring. "Oh, I worked third base today," Barnett said.

Barnett explained that they had four umpires in their camp. He was rooming with another umpire and was actually getting meal money so that he could eat in real restaurants without players harassing him. I was envious, and that phone call made me feel worse than I already did.

I got through spring training and then drove home to St. Louis for a few days before reporting for my first season in the minors. I was going to be working in the Class A Midwest League, covering the states of Illinois, Iowa, and Wisconsin.

Even though I was only home for a week or two, I needed a job—any job—to make some money. I answered an ad for a temporary job that looked pretty attractive. I put on a coat and tie like my dad taught me to do, found the downtown building, and walked into the lobby. It was just like the scene in the movie *On the Waterfront.* There were 50 or 60 guys in the building, all dressed in jeans and work boots, and they looked at me like I was one of the union representatives.

A man got up on the stage and started calling and pointing to different guys. He must have looked at me and thought, "Well look at that dumb SOB in the coat and tie." He pointed at me and emphatically yelled, "*You!*" I didn't know why I was being picked, but I was thrilled and happy because I would get a day's pay. I went with a group of guys and got in the back of a big box truck filled with Charmin toilet paper.

The job was to go out to the wealthy suburbs of St. Louis and walk door-to-door asking the resident of each house to try Charmin toilet paper. They dropped us off, and we couldn't come home until they picked us up. I got home about 7:00 P.M. and was just physically exhausted. I think I made $20 for the day.

I went to pick up Sharon, and I didn't know what I was going to say when she asked what I had done all day. "Well, I delivered toilet paper door-to-door." I didn't go back the next day.

Many years later, after Sharon and I had been married for more than 30 years, I was sitting with my father-in-law and I said, "Harry, I've got to ask you something." My father-in-law was not really a sports fan, and didn't know much about baseball, which was good for me, because that meant he never discussed sports. "Harry, you remember when Sharon and I were dating and were about to get married? There had to have been some quiet moments with you and Lois [his wife] when you said, 'I don't get this. Our daughter is going to marry a minor league umpire who is gone six months a year, makes $300 dollars a month for five months, and then comes home and doesn't have a job. What is this all about?' There had to have been some reservations about me marrying your daughter."

He thought for a minute and said, "No, Dave, we never had that discussion. I always thought that anybody who could lower himself to deliver toilet paper door-to-door was going to be successful somewhere, sometime, somehow."

Since I didn't make much money while working in the minor leagues, I began refereeing basketball games in church leagues and high schools to make a few extra dollars in the winter. Gene Barth, who went on to become an NFL referee for many years, suggested I referee college games; when I found I could make even more money doing that, I was hooked. I didn't have much time off, because the baseball and college basketball seasons were practically consecutive. If I didn't work any postseason baseball games, I could go home for October. But then the basketball season began in early November—while other umpires were sitting at home—and ran until March, when I would have to report for the start of spring training. If I was working the postseason tournaments, I barely got any time off at all. I remember one year I worked an Arizona at Arizona State game on March 3, and some of the A's who had gone to Arizona State, like Reggie Jackson and Sal Bando, were there. The next day I was umpiring their spring-training game.

I was fortunate to officiate for several conferences, including the Missouri Valley, Big Eight, Western Athletic, Sunbelt, and Metro conferences. Then I was promoted to supervisor of officials for the Metro, and later the Missouri Valley and Conference USA. In total, I worked for 17 years as supervisor of officials for those conferences. I was even asked to add my expertise as the color commentator for a couple of television broadcasts (although that took me a little bit out of my element).

Working in all of those conferences allowed me to spend time with some great coaches, including Norm Stewart, Bobby Knight, Jack Hartman, Bob Huggins, Denny Crum, Charlie Spoonhour, Lute Olson, Ray Meyer and his son Joey Meyer, Al McGuire, Frank McGuire, Gene Bartow, Hugh Durham, Eddie Fogler, Bill Foster, and even Dick Vitale (before he became an announcer). I also worked with and for Irv Brown, Johnny Overby, Jerry Lovelace, Jim Bain, and Bernie Saggau, very good people who also were influential to my career.

I was fortunate enough to be selected to work several tournaments in Hawaii; in December 1980 I worked an Indiana game there. Knight was the coach. There were about 18 seconds to go in the game, and Indiana had a comfortable lead, when my partner called a foul. There was a time-out, and when we were ready to shoot the free throws, my partner signaled that it was going to be one-and-one. Knight started screaming on the sideline, demanding that it should be two shots. I blew my whistle, walked right up to him, and gave him a good stern lecture, threatening to eject him immediately if he didn't sit down. He finally backed off and we finished the game.

The next day I looked at the schedule and saw that I had another Indiana game. I had a feeling that the tournament directors were trying to tell me, "If you can handle Earl Weaver and Billy Martin, we know you can handle Knight."

It was going to be the first game of the day, and some players were having their shoot-around on the court when I walked into the arena. The lights were on over the court, but the stands were dark. All of a sudden I heard a loud voice coming from the stands: "Hey, ref!" It was Knight, coming down from the stands and walking toward me in his wild sport coat.

"You're one of the major league umpires, aren't you?" he asked. When I said yes, he said, "Did you work the left-field line in the second game of the 1976 World Series?" I had to think about it for a minute, but then agreed that I had.

"I knew it," Knight said. "I knew I recognized you from someplace. I love baseball. Can we talk about baseball for a little while?"

I said sure and invited him to come to our dressing room.

Knight and I walked into the room just as my local Hawaiian partner was pulling on his pants; when that poor guy saw who I was with, he missed his pant leg, lost his balance, and fell to the floor. He was completely embarrassed, but also shocked that the legendary Knight was walking into our dressing room.

The three of us sat and talked baseball for about 20 minutes. Knight is a huge baseball fan and has been friends with several managers; he was particularly close to Sparky Anderson when Sparky was managing the Cincinnati Reds.

He is still big buddies with Tony LaRussa of the Cardinals, and he goes to several of their games each season.

Knight's team lost the game that night, but we did not have any problems with him. When the Hoosiers returned to the mainland, they didn't lose another game all season, and went on to win the 1981 NCAA championship.

My first umpiring contract was for $315 a month, plus seven cents a mile for travel expenses. I was getting married that winter, and the gas stations had a promotion that summer giving away dinnerware when you bought gas (which cost only 19 cents a gallon). I got the full complement of glasses, plates, bowls, and mixing bowls. That $315 didn't go very far, so we were always looking for deals like that.

My partner was a man named Larry Ellis, who lived in Springfield, Illinois. We stayed in a lot of bad hotels, but the worst hotel ever (which cost us $2 a night) was in Dubuque, Iowa.

Most of the people who stayed in that hotel were truck drivers. The bed barely fit in the room, and like most of the hotels we stayed in, there was no air-conditioning, no television in the room, and a common bathroom for all of the rooms in the hall. There was one black-and-white television in the lobby for everyone in the hotel.

We didn't have a dressing room at the park, so we had to keep our uniforms and sweaty equipment in our rooms. The odor was terrible. It smelled like a locker room. The first time I stayed there and went up to my room, I saw a rope curled up like a snake on the floor. It was tied to the radiator. When I went back to the desk, I asked the clerk what the rope was for. The clerk said calmly, "Oh, you throw that out the window if there is a fire. That's your fire escape."

Over the Fourth of July, my parents and Sharon came to a game in Appleton, Wisconsin, between Baltimore's farm team and Clinton, Iowa, the White Sox affiliate. It was the very first game Sharon saw me umpire. Ellis was working the plate, and I was on the bases.

Ellis always talked a lot between innings, and about the fifth or sixth inning, I saw Ellis and the catcher, Duane Josephson, start arguing about whether the pitcher could have a different ball. Don Bacon was the manager of the Clinton White Sox, and he came running out to intervene. Bacon was very upset and the argument was really starting to heat up.

I thought I had better try to be the peacemaker, so I started moving toward the argument. Before I got there, Ellis took off his mask, and he and Bacon bumped each other. When Bacon pushed Ellis away with his hands, it must have really upset Ellis, because what he did next was unbelievable. He swung his mask and hit Bacon in the mouth. Blood flew everywhere. The benches emptied and we had a real donnybrook going with everybody piling on Ellis. Billy DeMars, who was later a major league coach for many years, was managing Appleton, and thank God he helped. Together we finally got all of the players off Ellis.

Ellis was absolutely stunned. He was trying to act like nothing had happened and trying to get the game resumed. His whole uniform had been ripped off his back. I finally got him into the locker room and convinced him he couldn't continue. I took over and finished the game working by myself.

Ellis and Bacon both got suspended for 15 games, but I was the real victim. I had to work all those games with a local umpire every night, traveling by myself. The collection of fill-in umpires was amazing, including a guy who had a broken arm in a cast past his elbow.

My dad asked if I would like to have my 14-year-old brother, Greg, travel with me so that I wouldn't be by myself, and I thought that seemed like a good idea. Years later Greg told me that during games in Dubuque, my favorite town, he would sneak down to the locker room, get my car keys, and take off. He was driving my four-speed like a NASCAR driver while I was working the game. He knew when he had to get back, and I was so involved with my job I never had any idea what he was doing.

Another town in the league at that time was Waterloo, Iowa, the Red Sox affiliate. To get to the umpires' dressing room there, you had to go through the home team's clubhouse and crawl under the stands for about 25 feet through this little door.

One of the players on the team was Reggie Smith, who at that time was a third baseman, before he got to the big leagues as an outfielder with the Red Sox. Smith was having a tough time, making a lot of throwing errors, and when he kept arguing about a call, I ejected him. After the game, I had to go through the Red Sox clubhouse to get to my locker room. When I walked into the room, trying to hurry as much as possible, Smith was waiting for me. Luckily, all he did was scream obscenities until I was able to crawl to our room.

We crossed paths in the major leagues as well, but I don't know if he ever put two and two together and realized I was the same umpire who ran him in the Midwest League—even after I kicked him out of a game in the majors too.

A lot of the people I met in the minor leagues worked their way to the majors, both as managers and players. One manager was Chuck Tanner, whom I was with in the Midwest League and the Texas League. He was at Quad City in the Midwest League when I called one of his players out at second base during a game at Wisconsin Rapids in my second year.

One of the questions I get asked the most is what players and managers say when they come out to argue a call. A lot of times they are so upset they really aren't speaking in words. It's more like grunts and curse words all mixed together. In this case, however, when Tanner came running onto the field, I think he knew I had made the right call, but he also knew he had to come out to protect his player. When he got there, he got right in my face and started screaming: "Have I told you about the new restaurant downtown? You really ought to check it out. They've got great steaks." He was yelling, pointing his finger, and waving, and the crowd was going nuts because they thought he was really giving me hell about the call.

Larry Barnett was my partner in that game, and he asked me later why I didn't eject Tanner when he came out and appeared to argue so intently. I told him what Tanner had said, and Larry didn't believe me.

The next day when the managers came to home plate to exchange the lineup cards before the game, Tanner asked, "Hey, did you guys go to that restaurant?" I looked back at Larry and smiled as if to say, "See, what did I tell you?" Chuck continued, "I didn't want to argue; the kid was wrong. I just told him about that restaurant." Larry looked at me and still couldn't believe Chuck had really said that.

Larry had a big dispute one day with Walt Dixon, who was managing the Quincy Cubs. Dixon came out to argue a call, but he turned around and left almost as soon as he reached Larry. Between innings, Larry came out to me and said, "What does halitosis mean?" I said, "It means you have bad breath." Larry said, "Why that SOB." Naturally, Dixon thought he was being humorous.

Tanner also managed in the Texas League when I worked there, and of course later he managed in the major leagues. One day we were in Austin, Texas. Tanner was managing the El Paso team, and Austin was managed by Hub Kittle, who later became a pitching coach in the big leagues with Houston and the Cardinals.

My partner was Frannie Walsh, who had been a major league umpire years earlier but had gotten fired. He was at least 60 years old and needed a job, so the Texas League hired him.

Frannie and I were in our dressing room before the game, and Tanner came in, just visiting. He told Frannie that Kittle had called him an old man. Frannie really got upset, and when he went to home plate to exchange the lineups before the game, he said to Hub, "I understand you said I was an old man."

Hub looked at him like he didn't know what Frannie was talking about, but Frannie kept going. "Let me tell you something: if there is an old man here, it's you. Take your hat off." Frannie was screaming. Kittle, of course, was bald. At that point Tanner left. I think he was afraid he would die laughing. Hub took his hat off, and Frannie felt like he had won the argument, even though Kittle had no idea what he was referring to. "If there is anybody here who is old, it's you," said Frannie. "How do you like that, old man?" He was not trying to be funny—he was serious. If Hub had said one word, I know Frannie would have ejected him immediately.

Of all of the umpires I worked with, in both the majors and the minors, Frannie Walsh was one of the most unusual. Sadly, he is dead now. He made me laugh so hard in the three months we worked together that the tears would roll down my face. That was just Frannie.

Frannie would sit in his hotel room during the day, reading old letters and reminiscing about his short career in the majors, until it was time for the game. He would say, "Davey, did I read you this letter?" I'd say no, even though I had heard it 15 times, and Frannie would read it again and again.

I had to do all the driving, and one time we were sitting at a red light, and it seemed like the light was really taking a long time to change to green. Frannie got very upset and started screaming in the car. "What's wrong with this goddamn light?" Of course, we didn't have air-conditioning, so the windows were down and everybody in the cars near us could hear him screaming. But Frannie didn't care. He finally got out of the car, ran up to the stoplight, and started kicking the pole. "Change, you SOB," he yelled. I was laughing so hard, I cried—but again, he was dead serious. "Change, you SOB. Change."

One time we were in the car going someplace, and Frannie told me to make a U-turn. You had to do what he said, because otherwise he'd challenge you to a fight. So I made the turn, and a guy behind me started honking his horn. Frannie immediately leapt out of the car and started yelling at him. "Get out of that f****** truck and I'll kick your ass," he said. In a panic the driver rolled up his window very fast and refused to get out, looking at Frannie in fear and absolute disbelief. Once again, Frannie was serious.

With Frannie I never had time to be nervous before the games because I was always laughing so hard. We were driving from Austin to San Antonio one time, and we got a flat tire. We were on the side of the road changing it, when a big truck came flying by and scared both of us with the wind shear. Frannie was so mad, he had me drive 80 or 90 miles an hour to catch up with the guy.

Sure enough we finally caught him, and when we pulled up alongside of him, Frannie leaned out the window and yelled, "Pull this f****** truck over." I said, "Frannie, we can't stop. We've got to get to the game." I don't know what would have happened if we'd stopped. The driver had no idea what Frannie was screaming about; he looked at Frannie as if he was crazy. Sometimes I wondered the same thing, but I always loved him.

I think all the players and most of the managers were scared of him on the field. There were some good managers in the league, like Tanner, Kittle, Pete Reiser, Bob Kennedy, and Vern Rapp. There were good players, and even some older players from Frannie's time, in the league. But of all of them Tanner was the best at egging Frannie on.

"Frannie, I'm sure glad we've got you. I sure love to see you work," he would say before the game. Frannie would never do anything special for him, but he loved hearing that.

Tanner's El Paso team was playing Rapp's Arkansas club. Frannie was behind the plate; I was on the bases. There was a checked-swing call, and Rapp asked for the appeal. Frannie stopped and pointed to me and said emphatically, "Davey, did he go?" I yelled no and gave the safe sign. Rapp then started yelling at me. "You didn't see it either," he said. Frannie came out from behind the plate and ran all the way to the dugout in a rage. He almost fell into the dugout before he was able to stop. "You asked me to ask and I asked," he yelled at Rapp. "If you've got something to say, you say it to me." Rapp said calmly, "I'm not talking to you, Frannie," and Frannie screamed back, "Well, I'm talking to you." Rapp said, "You will run me if I do," and Frannie said, "You bet your life I will." Tears were rolling down my face as I tried not to look like I was laughing.

Frannie always hustled on the field, and he was really an aggressive umpire. He was always challenging players and managers. Frannie had their respect, and they were scared. I was convinced that that was the way you were supposed to umpire. However, I forgot I had a baby face and was a 22-year-old kid, and he was a former major league umpire. He looked like an umpire, too: mean, old, and tough.

I was behind the plate in Amarillo one time when the pitcher didn't like a call, and he looked in at me. I went out from behind the plate and ripped my mask off like Frannie would have. I yelled back at him, he said something back, and I threw him out of the game. Frannie took me aside after the game and asked if I really thought I needed to throw the pitcher out of the game. I was a little put off by that because I was trying to do it like he did. But I realized that I was young and learning, and there was a time to be strong and tough, but there were also other ways to handle different situations. Frannie was a good teacher and confidence builder.

I was promoted to the Triple A International League the next year, and I continued to emulate Frannie's style. That was a gigantic mistake. The players were scared of Frannie, but they weren't scared of me. My yelling with a demonstrative attitude didn't look the same as his did, especially at the Triple A level with managers such as Earl Weaver, Don Zimmer, and Luman Harris. It was the wrong time and place for someone without any experience or credibility to use that aggressive style. About the middle of that first season I realized that approach was good for Frannie but not good for me, so I changed, luckily before it was too late.

One of my partners in the International League was Tom Ravashiere, and he was a truly great umpire. He should have made the major leagues but never did except as a replacement during the 1979 strike. He had been featured in a big story in *Life* magazine about the life of a minor league umpire. He had a wonderful style of umpiring, and he enjoyed his job.

He also was the kind of guy who liked to show he was the boss, especially if somebody had challenged him. One day in a game in Jacksonville, the batter was Bobby Mitchell, a guy who was always complaining, so Tom decided he was going to teach him a lesson. He got my attention, then motioned to the catcher to move outside for the pitch. He promptly called it strike one.

I was standing at second base, and I knew exactly what was going on. I was trying my hardest not to start laughing. On the next pitch, he hit the catcher, Del Bates, on the shoulder and motioned to him to get even farther outside. Strike two.

Mitchell was furious, but he knew he couldn't say anything because Tom had given him a similar lesson before. Tom was standing there, not paying any attention to Mitchell staring at him. Bates moved outside again, and Tom ended Mitchell's misery by calling strike three.

This time Mitchell went crazy, and Tom said just one word—"*out*"—and pointed to the clubhouse. It was a classic ejection. Clyde McCullough was the manager, and he came out to argue. Tom didn't like Clyde either, so he put his mask on and got right in Clyde's face, screaming and scraping Clyde's face with the mask. It went on for quite a while. Rav walked away abruptly, and Clyde naturally followed. Rav suddenly stopped and with his elbow stuck out, turned and buried it in Clyde's stomach. Clyde doubled over, and Rav left him there writhing in pain. All of this was totally legal, I might add. Clyde never fooled with him again.

What I really learned at that level was that one of the toughest parts of being an umpire is learning how to handle people. Good people skills are as important as all of the other duties and responsibilities of an umpire if he is going to be successful. It's a difficult thing to control 18 individuals, plus the managers, who are highly skilled at what they do, and you know that any time you make a call, half of them are going to disagree with you.

I learned early in my career that umpiring is not a popularity contest. You have to be able to handle people and gain their respect at the same time.

One of the people who helped me learn that, surprisingly enough, was none other than Earl Weaver. He was managing Rochester, Baltimore's top farm team. I was well aware of him because he had been a minor leaguer in the Cardinals' system and I had seen him play in games that my dad umpired.

My dad didn't like the fact that I kind of liked Earl as a player because of his fiery and aggressive style. I know my dad had to eject him a number of times during his career.

I knew Earl's background, but I never told him that my dad had been an umpire in the minor leagues, and I never knew until years later whether he made the connection between us or not. After Earl retired, we were once together at a charity golf tourament where I heard him tell several people that "Dave's dad threw me out of games." That's when I became aware that he knew of the connection—but he told me he knew who I was the first day I showed up in the International League.

People who only saw Earl manage in the major leagues missed the real show. I told Dick Butler, the supervisor of umpires in the American League for many years, that I owed part of my reputation as a good umpire to Earl Weaver. "Earl who?" he asked. He couldn't believe the Earl we both knew would actually *help* an umpire.

"Earl Weaver," I said. "We had so many arguments in the International League. By learning how to handle Earl I figured out how to handle negative situations. The SOB gave you everything you thought you could possibly get, and just when you thought he was done he'd get going again."

Earl was brutal in the minors. He would get so mad about a call he would pick up the base and go lock himself in his dressing room. It was the minors, so they didn't have another base. The groundskeeper would have to knock on the door and beg him to give the base back so that we could continue the game.

Everybody at the Triple A level—the players, the managers, and the umpires—is really only thinking about one thing: what he has to do to get to the next level, the major leagues.

Mike Ferraro was a third baseman for Syracuse, the Yankees' top club, and he got called up for a short stay. I was standing near him not long after he was sent back to Syracuse and was eager to know what it was like in the majors.

"Man, Davey, I was so nervous," he said. "Mickey said to me [and I knew he meant Mickey Mantle] that when this one older umpire is working, no matter what he calls, you don't look at him, don't talk to him, and don't acknowledge him because he will screw you until you can't walk." Ferraro told me the umpires made the rookies walk a fine line. I found out later that umpires in the forties, fifties, and sixties said, "If you didn't like that call, wait until you see the next one."

There were umpires, especially the older guys, who umpired entirely by intimidation. Luckily that has changed over the years, I think in part because of television. The replays show whether an umpire made the correct call, and guys who are consistently wrong are told to find something else to do for a living.

I spent four years in the International League and was getting disenchanted and impatient because I had not received a shot at the major leagues. I came back to St. Louis one winter and got a job selling typewriters, seeing if I would like doing something else, because I was starting to question whether or not I would ever make it to the major leagues.

Finally, I got a phone call in July of 1970 from Barney Deary with the news that the National League was going to purchase my contract in November at the winter meetings, which was the way it was usually done. I called Sharon and we were both unbelievably excited.

However, two weeks later I was in Louisville having dinner with Sharon when Dick Butler walked right past our table. Butler was the A.L. supervisor of umpires at that time. I knew him from the Texas League, but I wasn't positive it was him, so I went to a lobby phone and asked for the room of Dick Butler. The operator started to connect me and I hung up. I just wanted to make sure it was him.

Dick called me early the next morning and asked me to meet him for breakfast. He told me the American League was going to purchase my contract. I don't know if I said it or not, but I know the thought went through my head: "Oh my." Finally I worked up the nerve to tell him that I really appreciated it but I had already been told that I was going to the National League. But Butler said the American League decided they wanted me and that they were purchasing my contract in August, even though I wasn't going to begin working games until the next season. I was confused but very happy to know for sure that I was going to my version of Disney World—the major leagues.

My last minor league assignment was the Little World Series, between Omaha and Syracuse in 1970. The series was supposed to open in Omaha, but after three days of rain, they moved the games to Syracuse. They were supposed to play the first couple of games there and then move back to Omaha, but it turned out they played four games in Syracuse, and Syracuse won all four, sweeping the series. Some of the Omaha players were on the same flight I was on the next day, and they were really criticizing the Omaha general manager, Bob Quinn, for allowing all the games to be played in Syracuse. He had to sit there and take their abuse. Bob Quinn and I have been good friends from that day on.

Omaha was managed by Jack McKeon, a longtime major league manager. Jack told me one of the most unbelievable stories I have ever heard about the minor leagues, and he swears it is true.

Jack was a player/manager with Missoula, Montana, in the Class C Pioneer League in the late fifties. He was the catcher, and they had one out in the inning with a runner on third. The batter hit a fly ball to left, which was caught. The runner on third tagged up and tried to score just as the ball was coming in from the outfield. Jack said it was a bang-bang play, and after a long wait, the umpire called the runner safe.

Jack went nuts and argued, and the umpire said, "Well, Jack, it was a really close play. I really think it probably was a tie."

Jack said, "You can't have a tie in baseball. If it was a tie, we should do it over."

After a long argument, the umpire was perplexed, and obviously inexperienced, and finally said OK. Despite the strong disagreement of the other manager, they finally put the runner back on third, gave the ball to the left fielder, and signaled when the runner should go. He was thrown out by 20 feet, in the only "do over" I have ever heard of in professional baseball.

After those seven years in the minor leagues, I had heard and experienced a lot, but my career was really just beginning. I was on my way to the major leagues.

3

Crazy Nights

My grandmother lived near the old Busch Stadium in St. Louis, and when I rode the bus to her house, I always checked the Cardinals' schedule on the bus advertisements, hoping they would be playing a doubleheader. I went to as many games as my mom could afford and once in a while I got free tickets from umpires who had worked in the minors with my dad.

One of those umpires was Stan Landes, a big, tough, gruff man whom the Cardinals hated, especially Solly Hemus. He called and asked my mom if I would like to go to a game with him. He waited for my mom to drop me off in front of the stadium. I was a typical 10-year-old kid and therefore his gruffness and demeanor scared me. He was still gruff, but he was very nice to me. He walked me into the stadium and asked if I wanted a hot dog, an orange soda, or potato chips. I said no, because my mom always instructed me to never ask for or accept anything. I told him I had my own money, but he ignored my answer and went over to the concession stand and bought me everything—a hot dog, chips, an orange soda, and a program. Then he walked me down to my seat, made sure I was OK, and gave me $3 to spend. I never forgot how kind he was to me because I am sure he knew my mom did not have a lot of money to give me for concessions.

Years later I actually worked with Stan in spring training. Although Stan said he didn't remember doing that, I never forgot.

Stan was fired in 1972, unfortunately, but I always called him and made sure he had tickets, souvenirs, and anything I could do for him to show him my respect and friendship.

Even though I had traveled with my dad to many minor league games outside of St. Louis, I had never been to another major league stadium. Working the night shift in a factory in the early sixties, I listened on the radio to Cardinals games on the West Coast and always dreamed of what those stadiums must be like.

I had worked in the minor leagues for seven years and never made more than $500 a month. After Sharon and I were married, our tax man actually refused to prepare our tax returns one year because he knew I had to be cheating and not reporting all of my income. "You had to make more money than that," he told me. He was wrong.

When my contract was purchased by the American League and I found out I was going to make $10,000 a year, we thought we were wealthy.

There had been some talk about wanting me to work major league games in September of 1970, but I had never used the outside chest protector when working home plate in the minors, and it was still required in the A.L. Although I would have liked to have gone up in September—and somebody in the league office said I could just work the bases, rotating between crews—I was glad they abandoned that idea. The senior umpires would have marked me for life as a base umpire. Instead, the league sent me to the Instructional League for a month after the season ended to learn how to use the outside protector.

I was assigned to a crew headed by Larry Napp for the 1971 season. Larry had been in the American League since 1951 and had worked four World Series, and I was excited to work with him. I was 26, and when we walked out of the stadium together after games, some fans would shout, "Hey, Larry, good to see you've got your son with you." In those days umpires seemed old, gray, fat, and bald, and I was none of those at that time. Hell, I had a baby face. Napp also had some senior moments. Even after we had been working and traveling together for several months, he still couldn't remember my name. When friends of his made that comment about me being his son, he would say, "Oh, no, this is my partner." He would stammer and stutter, and could not introduce me properly because he had forgotten my name. I learned quickly to stick out my hand and say, "Dave Phillips, nice to meet you."

My first big-league game was in Anaheim, and I worked third base. I remember walking onto the field, standing there, and realizing that even if I got fired tomorrow, I had at least been a major league umpire for one day. Luckily that didn't happen and I was able to have a wonderful 32-year career that produced many great memories.

I will never forget driving to the game in Anaheim that first day. Napp was sitting in the front seat, and he was wearing a World Series ring. While I was in the minors, I used to ask God for a chance to work in the majors. I said it was all I'd ever ask for. Larry took off his ring so I could get a closer look at it, and I said a silent prayer to myself: "God, if I could only get one of these, that would be all I would ever ask." I got one six years later, and after 30 minutes of admiring it, I said, "God, I wonder if I could get two of these rings . . ."

During my time, I have witnessed some incredible things on baseball fields. I have met and become good friends with fans, players, managers, general managers, and legends of the game. I was able to travel; I have experienced some unbelievable moments and incredible athletic achievements. And a lot of crazy stuff happened along the way.

One of my partners during the 1973 season was Ron Luciano, and he was a very unusual and extremely funny person. Everything he did was funny. Ronnie was truly a showman. He was the only umpire I knew whom people paid to watch umpire, and by God he was determined to give them a show—he was going to entertain them. He would walk out of the tunnel from our dressing room, sometimes feeling absolutely terrible, and give the crowd a big salute with both arms raised as if he were Richard Nixon walking onto the stage to give a speech.

Ronnie kept a bottle of Maalox in his locker, and there were nights when he was slumped in a chair and you could just tell he didn't feel well. He was a big man, and kind of gawky, and he would just take that bottle of Maalox and gulp it down. Forget about the two tablespoons or whatever you were supposed to take. He did it one night in Cleveland, right before we went on the field. I know he felt terrible. At the old stadium in Cleveland you had to walk down a long ramp to get to the field, then climb up a set of steps. He had problems with his knees too, and it was tough for him to get up those steps. But he got no farther than the top step before he saw the people waiting for him, and suddenly all his problems were forgotten. The show was on.

Ronnie and I had gone to umpiring school together, and we were friends. He was a much more demonstrative umpire than anyone else who ever umpired, and his actions made him extremely popular with the press, which in turn made him famous and popular with the fans. He was always being rated as one of the top umpires in the league, but in reality that wasn't quite true—because Ronnie was just as interested in how he was calling a play as he was in getting the call right.

Ronnie, who had played football at Syracuse University, was always talking about food. He loved great restaurants, and every night he would decide where we were going to eat after the game. He would ask the other umpires what kind of food they wanted, and then he would look up that type of cuisine, call up the restaurant to make sure they had it, and that's where we went that night. Ronnie was a wonderful person to spend time with, and I always laughed and enjoyed his company whenever I was with him.

In truth, Ronnie overdid everything. He ran like crazy, he ate too much, he looked funny; everybody laughed and he laughed with them. He truly was an entertainer more than he ever was an umpire.

I remember working in Cleveland one day, and Ronnie had the plate. I was working first base. Ken Aspromonte was managing the Indians, and they were playing Oakland. Campy

Campaneris was the leadoff batter, and as the pitcher began his windup for the first pitch of the game, I immediately noticed that Ron was not wearing a mask. He was in his crouch behind the catcher, the pitch was on its way to home plate, and Ron did not have his mask on.

I started to raise my arms and call time, but the pitcher had already thrown the pitch. Campaneris tried to do his famous run-and-bunt play, but he fouled off the ball. Aspromonte had seen me raise my arms, and he came out of the dugout as I came down the line toward the plate. Ken thought I was calling Campaneris out for being out of the batter's box when I had thrown my arms up. He either didn't realize or didn't care that Luciano had forgotten his mask.

I ran in to the plate and said, "Ron, do you know you don't have your mask?"

"Damn, I knew there had to be a reason why I was seeing the pitch much better," Luciano said.

Another time, we were in Chicago for a game, and one of the television networks had him wired with a microphone to tape him for a special they were going to air about his antics on the field. He was working first base and I was at second, and he kept coming over to talk to me. At one point he had to make a call on a ball hit down the right-field line, and he came over to explain to me that he wanted to call it fair but didn't because of the fifty-five thousand people in the stands cheering for the White Sox. I was shocked and motioned to him that he was wearing a microphone, hoping he would remain quiet, but he didn't care. In fact, he had said it on purpose to create a good show for the television special. He was always saying things like that intentionally; he loved controversy.

I remember there was a close play at second in the same game, and the manager was coming out to argue. Here came Ronnie, running as hard as he could toward me, waving his arms and screaming, "Great call, Davey! Great call!" I just started laughing. That's the kind of stuff he would do. The manager just walked away, shaking his head.

Ron and Earl Weaver had some serious altercations when Weaver was managing the Orioles. Their feud went way back to the minor leagues. Once Ron ejected Weaver in both games of a doubleheader. When the reporters came into our locker room after the second game, they asked Ronnie if he was holding a grudge against Weaver. "Oh no," Ronnie said. "I just want you all to know that when I umpire, I never care who wins the game as long as *the Orioles don't.*" The reporters were shocked and stunned, so they repeated the question to Ron and he said the same thing exactly the same way. I couldn't believe it.

He drove the league officials absolutely crazy. They would call and scream at him. He would say how sorry he was and tell them it wouldn't happen again. Then, of course, the same thing would happen the next night.

Ron also had a feud with Billy Martin. He told the league he would never umpire games when Martin was managing because he felt the league was not disciplining Martin enough. We went to Texas, where Billy was managing the Rangers, and true to his word Ronnie stayed home all three games. We worked with a three-man crew. Those kinds of incidents really didn't endear him to league officials, but he was never fired and didn't care.

Ron liked Mickey Stanley, who at the time was playing center field for the Detroit Tigers. One game, Ron was working second base, but instead he stood in center field, 200 feet away, next to Stanley. "How do you play this guy?" he said. He then proceeded to carry on a continual conversation throughout the game. If there was a play at second, the umpire working third had to come over and make the call.

Jim Campbell was the general manager of the Tigers, and he was furious. Jim was always Mr. Law and Order, and he wanted everything done by the book. He called and screamed at somebody in the league office, but I think it had gotten to the point that those calls didn't faze the league anymore. Ron was a major problem and they couldn't deal with him.

One thing that Ronnie did throughout his career was remember that the game should be fun. Whether he was tossing a make-believe grenade into a dugout or eating a hot dog with the fans, Ronnie had a good time every time he went on the field. He really was better than Max Patkin, the Clown Prince of Baseball. He would walk over to the stands and get a hot dog or a Coke from a vendor. He made the fans laugh and the league officials cringe. I didn't have time to worry about the game around Ronnie because we were always laughing so hard.

NBC had the television rights to the baseball *Game of the Week* in those days, and they thought enough of Ronnie's personality that they hired him to become an announcer. When Ron called the A.L. office to tell them he was quitting, he said he thought he actually heard champagne corks popping in the background.

Ronnie wasn't the only umpire who had problems with Weaver. Weaver was involved in the worst argument I ever had on the field during the worst weekend of my career, a four-game series between the Yankees and the Orioles in Baltimore in August 1978. It was a series from hell.

The Baltimore Colts shared the stadium with the Orioles in those days, and since the football season had begun, the field was always in terrible shape once the Colts played a couple of games. The nightmare started on a Friday night. We had to stop the game several times because of rain. Water always collected in left field because of the football damage to the field, and it quickly became a lake. The water was ankle deep, and I thought I saw a fish jump. It literally was so deep that if the ball went in there you were not going to find it. We finally had to call the game after the sixth inning, and the Yankees won 2–1. Naturally, Weaver was upset because he thought we could still play. It always amazed me how the team that was losing never thought the game should be called (especially when the loser was somebody like Earl).

The Saturday game was even worse. We started on time but had three or four rain delays, and then shockingly the lights went out, not once but three times. I was working first base, and in the sixth inning I called a balk on Mike Flanagan, the Orioles' pitcher. Weaver of course came out to argue, and I ejected him, as usual. Weaver had a habit of putting his hat on real hard so it wouldn't fall off during an argument. When he went nose to chest with umpires, he would beak the umpire with the bill of the cap, like a bird. He had never done that to me, but I had seen him do it to others. Earl was really upset, as usual, and I was just as aggravated. I warned him, "I'm going to tell you something, Earl. You beak me with that hat and I'm going to knock you on your ass." I was dead serious, and I believe I would have done it, because as I said the series really was awful. He didn't do it, thankfully, but before he and I finished arguing, some of the coaches actually dragged him off the field. I must admit I didn't use my people skills that time, but that made us even— neither did Earl.

After the very long argument, Lou Piniella happened to be the next batter, and Lou disliked Weaver from having played for him in the minors. Lou hit a routine ground ball to second. Rich Dauer bobbled it, which made it a close play, but Lou was clearly out. I had no more than signaled him out when he went absolutely nuts. Fortunately for me, first-base coach Gene Michael, manager Bob Lemon, and several players jumped on him and held him on the ground. That was the only time in my career I actually thought I was going to be punched by a player. If he got loose, I was going to take off running toward right field.

Naturally, I ejected him too. Within two pitches, I had ejected Weaver and Piniella, from opposing teams. After the game, I found out that when Lou got back in the clubhouse, he was still extremely upset. He asked one of the clubhouse attendants if the replay showed he was out. The kid tried to ignore him and was scared to tell him, knowing Lou's hot temper. After Lou asked several times, the kid said, "Yeah, Lou, I saw the replay and it looked like you were out." The kid thought Piniella would start tearing up the clubhouse with that news, but instead he just sat in front of his locker and said calmly, "Yeah, I thought so."

The next day, Sunday afternoon, I had the plate, and I had made up my mind not to listen to anything from anybody. The game was scoreless going into the sixth inning, and it started raining again. The field was already soaked from the past two days, so we knew it wasn't going to take much rain to make it unplayable.

The Orioles scored three times in the sixth to take a 3–0 lead. The Yankees rallied for five runs in the top of the seventh, making the score 5–3. It was still raining as we began the bottom of the seventh, and I knew we had to get three outs or the Yankees' runs would not count. Goose Gossage came in to pitch and was taking his time getting warmed up, and Graig Nettles was yelling at him to hurry up as the rain got more intense. I think Nettles might have been the only guy on the field who knew the rule.

We couldn't get the inning in. We had to stop the game. The ground crew covered the infield, and after 45 minutes, left field was flooded again, just as it had been two nights earlier. It was obvious we were going to have to call the game and the Orioles were going to win. Weaver had kept saying we could play when left field was under water Friday night, when the Orioles were behind. He said we could use towels to mop up the water. We went out to left field and I yelled at him to come with us. He trotted out like he was my little buddy.

"Earl, I'm going to tell you what we are going to do," I said. "I want you to get those f****** towels and get your ass out here and mop this f****** water up like you told me we could do Friday, because we are going to play this game."

He said, "What are you talking about? We can't play with this lake."

"Well, you told me Friday night we could play if we could get towels and mop up the lake. Well, go get the f****** towels and let's see you mop it up," I said. Earl said, nicely I might add, "Davey, why do you treat me this way?"

I said, "Because you are an unfair SOB."

He left, and we waited a short while, then called the game. Because the rule at the time was the score had to revert back to the last completed inning, the Orioles won 3–0. Ed Figueroa was the losing pitcher for the Yankees. We found out later he went into the umpires' dressing room and dumped coffee all over Don Denkinger's clothes.

The Yankees protested, and their owner, George Steinbrenner, was so upset that he led the campaign to have the rule changed that winter, saying that if a team scored in the top of an inning and then the game was stopped, it became a suspended game. The game then would be resumed and completed from that point, instead of becoming a complete game called after the last full inning. I don't think I ever agreed on anything with George, but that was certainly a much better and fairer rule.

Unfortunately, the series continued on Monday, and ABC was broadcasting the game. Howard Cosell was there and he interviewed Don, who was the crew chief. We had two more rain delays and another power failure that night, but at least there were no more arguments. At the time, the Yankees were eight games out, but they went on to tie Boston for the American League East title and have their playoff game (in which Bucky Dent hit his famous home run). That might never have happened if the Yankees hadn't lost that game because of the rain on Sunday.

There were a lot of managers like Weaver in the seventies. Billy Martin was the same kind of manager, as was Dick Williams. They challenged and tried to intimidate umpires, and continued until they realized they were not going to be successful.

My first few years in the league, Martin tried to do it to me. I changed that in 1974, during a four-game series in Texas. I was working third base, and I watched as Martin got all over Lou DiMuro in the first game. The Rangers yelled at Lou unmercifully through the whole game. The next night, Jim Odom was behind the plate and the same thing happened. I worked first base the third night, with Bill Deegan behind the plate. It wasn't as bad, but Martin was still yelling.

I had the plate for the fourth game, and I had made up my mind that if he yelled at me I was going to eject him. I thought about the situation, and I knew he was Billy Martin and I was still a young umpire, but I was determined not to let him intimidate me. He was not going to yell at me because I was not going to tolerate it. If he yelled at me about anything, he was going to be ejected.

We got to the seventh inning and not one word had been said. I admit I was listening intently for Billy. Finally he couldn't resist any longer. I called a pitch on Cesar Tovar that he didn't like. He started complaining. I turned around and stared at Martin in the dugout. "Are you talking to me?" I yelled. "If you've got any guts, you will come out here and talk to me."

I had no more gotten out the words *guts* and *to me* when Billy arrived at the plate. He was right in my face. "What do you mean if I have any guts," he was screaming. I yelled right back. I said terrible things, but it honestly was the way you had to deal with those guys back then. It was the only thing they understood.

He bumped my chest protector. "Go ahead and bump me," I yelled, "because I'm going to get your f****** ass suspended, you no-good SOB."

Obviously I ejected him, and even as Martin was leaving, I was still steaming. Jim Fregosi, who was nearing the end of his career and who I know liked Martin, came out to warm up a new pitcher, and he started talking to me.

"I'm really proud of you," Fregosi said. "Don't bend. Don't ever take that kind of crap. You really showed me something."

We finished the game, but I still had not calmed down. I was determined not to put up with that kind of abuse. Dick Butler, the supervisor of umpires, was at the game, and I waited for him to come into our dressing room after the game. Evidently Dick knew how upset I was, because he never showed up.

After an off day, our crew went to Boston for two games. Then we had another off day before a weekend series in Baltimore. I had to go to Baltimore on that off day because Butler had asked me to go in early and explain to Earl Weaver and Dave McNally why I had called McNally for a balk a few weeks earlier.

When I checked into the hotel, there was a letter waiting for me. That was not unusual, but I did a little double take when I saw it was from the Texas Rangers. I opened it while I was standing at the desk. I was shocked. It was from Billy Martin.

It started off with him talking about how he had considered me a good umpire. I didn't know if Martin even knew who I was, let alone if I was a good umpire. Then he addressed my comments about him not having any guts.

"If you think I'm gutless, I will be more than willing to meet you on any street in America," Martin wrote. I was standing there thinking, "You've got to be kidding me." I couldn't believe he had written this letter to me.

As I said, I had to go to the stadium to see McNally and Weaver, and the best thing about it for me was that Bill Haller's crew was in town working the game. I had told Haller earlier what I had to do, and he offered to go see Weaver and McNally with me. I really appreciated it.

As I got to the stadium and started walking down the hallway toward the umpires' dressing room, who should happen to walk around the corner toward the dugout but Billy Martin. His back was to me, but I knew it was him. I yelled, "Hey, Martin, here I am." I was really just kidding, but the noise echoed off the walls and it was very loud. He turned around and glared, but I could tell he didn't know who I was. I was in street clothes, and the hallway was poorly lit, and he didn't know me that well anyway.

As I walked closer, really not knowing what was going to happen, he finally realized who I was. "Why you little SOB," he said and grabbed me by the back of my neck, smiling as he did it. I kept on walking into the umpires' dressing room, and he came with me.

"I really like you," he said to me.

Haller was in the room, sitting and smoking his pipe, and Martin started in with him. "Billy, this little SOB told me I was gutless," Martin said. Haller just sat there laughing and calmly said, "Billy, leave the kid alone."

The whole episode was unbelievable. I had not gone out there to see Martin, and I think he knew that. When I told him why I was there, he started bad-mouthing Weaver. I really think having Haller there to reassure Martin that I was a good umpire went a long way toward developing Martin's opinions about me.

Umpires had to challenge managers in those days. That was the way managers talked to umpires, by cursing, and that's the way the game was played and officiated. Every other word was a curse word. Players chewed tobacco, spit, ate hamburgers, and drank beer. Only a few games were on television, and nobody—other than Luciano—was ever miked. It isn't like that today, and umpires are taught coming up through the minor leagues not to curse. It's far more sophisticated now, and that's no doubt a much better atmosphere to work in.

There have been a lot of managers in the majors who were hopelessly out of their league. One of them was Maury Wills, the former Dodgers star who took over the Seattle Mariners in 1980.

Maury was a nice guy, but I couldn't believe it one day when we came out to home plate before a game at the Kingdome to exchange the lineup cards. I could feel that something was not right, but I couldn't figure out what it was. It was like when you walk into your house and your wife has rearranged the furniture. You can just tell something isn't right. I said, "This batter's box looks bigger." Wills came out and said, very innocently, "We've been working on drag bunts and the guys were having a hard time staying in the batter's box, so I had the ground crew make it longer." I was so stunned I laughed. I couldn't believe what Wills had just said.

Wills was shocked when I told him he couldn't do that because it was against the rules. We had to delay the start of the game while the crew came out and redid the boxes.

Of course, Wills was the same manager who once came out on his second trip to the mound in an inning to change pitchers when he had nobody warming up in the bullpen. He also left a spring-training game in the sixth inning one day because he was flying to Los Angeles to meet somebody for dinner.

As crazy as that seems, the worst example of a poor decision that I ever was involved in on the field came in 1979, when the Chicago White Sox and their innovative owner, Bill Veeck, staged a promotion that just had disaster written all over it. And that's exactly what Disco Demolition Night became—a disaster.

The White Sox were playing Detroit in a doubleheader on July 12. Umpires never pay much attention to promotions that are planned at a game unless we read about them in the newspaper. I might have read something about this, but I really don't remember. If I did, it certainly didn't prepare me for the night to come.

I was working the plate in the first game, and I noticed about the fifth or sixth inning that an unusually large crowd seemed to be building. The bleachers were getting full, the upper deck was filling up, and some of the fans were sailing music records onto the field like Frisbees. We had to stop the game several times to pick them up. I had to ask the public-address announcer to make a plea for fans not to throw any more records onto the field. I suppose I should have been aware of the potential problems this posed for the second game, but I really was just trying to make sure we finished the first game.

We did, with Detroit winning 4–1. Everybody left the field, and we told the two teams to be ready for the second game in 30 minutes.

I took a quick shower, all of the umpires got something to eat, and we relaxed until the time the second game was supposed to start. My old partner, Nestor Chylak, was at the game as a supervisor in the locker room. There was absolutely no concern about what was going on out on the field, and nobody came to tell us we were about to have a major problem.

It turned out the promotion was being run in conjunction with a Chicago radio station, WLUP-FM. What I didn't know was that the promotion allowed fans who brought a disco record with them to be admitted to the game for 98 cents. Everybody who brought a record was then going to be allowed onto the field between games, at which time they would put the records into a giant Dumpster in center field to be blown up. That was the demolition part of Disco Demolition Night.

I don't know what kind of crowd the White Sox and the radio station expected to get, but I suspect it wasn't anything near the number of people who showed up—more than fifty thousand.

After the 30 minutes had expired since the end of the first game, the other three umpires and I walked out of our dressing room, ready for the second game. As soon as we got out the door, we were met by a Chicago police officer. He was standing between our door and the White Sox dugout. He turned around and looked at us and said, "Where do you guys think you're going?"

We told him we were the umpires, but he just shook his head. "Have you seen the field? There is no way you are going to play this game on time."

He told us we would be better off going out the other door of our dressing room and into the stands. Then we would have

Here I am during my time in the minor leagues with my partner at the time, Frannie Walsh. Frannie kept me in stitches much of the time we worked together, but I found out the hard way that it wasn't a good idea for me to emulate his fiery, aggressive umpiring style so early in my career.

Making a strike call during my minor league years; this happened to be a 17-inning game.

My father, Bob Phillips, working behind the plate in a Triple A game. I've been told many times that he should have worked in the major leagues, but he never got that opportunity.

This is my first official photo taken after the American League hired me in 1971.

Here I am involved in what looks like a minor disagreement with legendary Orioles manager Earl Weaver. People don't believe me when I tell them that I owe a lot of my success to Earl. Through numerous encounters like this one, he really taught me how to handle myself in tough situations. Larry McCoy is on my right and Don Denkinger is behind me.

The first ejection of my career was none other than Reggie Jackson, whom I consider to be the greatest clutch hitter I ever saw. Reggie and I actually became good friends over the years, and after this—his final game at Fenway Park—he signed his bat and gave it to me as a gift.

My first of many run-ins with Billy Martin happened when he was managing the Texas Rangers. Despite our differences, we almost immediately developed a lasting mutual respect—mainly because I didn't back down from him.

July 12, 1979, is one of the more memorable nights of my career, but for all the wrong reasons. A White Sox promotion called Disco Demolition Night went haywire, resulting in this mob scene and actual fires in the outfield. The White Sox were forced to forfeit the second game of the doubleheader because the field was unplayable. PHOTO COURTESY OF AP/WIDE WORLD PHOTOS.

Speaking of disco, that's me in the white shoes with crew members Bill Haller (left) and Jerry Neudecker, relaxing before a game.

It was just my luck to end up being the umpire who tossed famed spitballer Gaylord Perry for the first time in his 21-year career in 1982. It was seat-cushion night in Seattle, and the fans really let me have it.

Red Sox second baseman Jerry Remy, now a television broadcaster for the team, always had a way with words.

Here I am at the center of another famous ejection of a pitcher for doctoring the ball. Above, we're collecting several scuffed baseballs thrown by Joe Niekro (below), who denied any wrongdoing even after we found part of an emery board on him (notice his back pockets turned inside out).

a better idea of what was going on. We did, and to our shock, nobody was in the stands—everybody was on the field.

I have never seen anything like it. Center field was literally on fire. Some of the fans who had not deposited their records into the giant hopper had started their own small fires to burn the records. Home plate had been dug up. The bases were gone. People were lying all over the field smoking marijuana. You could smell it. We sat down in the stands and watched in dismay.

Harry Caray was broadcasting for the White Sox in those days, and he was as popular there as he later was with the Cubs. He came on the big video board and pleaded with his unique voice for the fans to clear the field so that we could play the second game. "Come on, fans, this is Harry Caray. We've got a game to play. Let's get going," he said. The people ignored him or yelled at him to go to hell or gave him the finger.

The promotion was supposed to take 15 minutes, but it had now been more than an hour. The Chicago police finally showed up in riot gear, with dogs, and charged onto the field. Finally the people began to move. If the cops had turned those dogs loose, those people would have been eaten alive. They got the field cleared.

It was now my duty as crew chief to walk around the field and see what kind of shape it was in. It was obvious the field was in no condition for a game. Sparky Anderson had just become the Tigers' manager, and he made it clear that he didn't want to play in these conditions. In addition to the status of the field, it was a riotous situation because the fans in the stands were drunk or high or both, and there was no telling what they would do during the game.

We made the decision to cancel the game because of the unplayable conditions. We were back in our dressing room when Veeck came charging in, pleading with us not to cancel the game. "We can play this goddamn game," he said. "Give me 15 minutes. We will have the field ready."

"Bill, we can't do it," I said. I sensed this promotion was going to be an embarrassing situation for him and his team, and the room got really quiet. All of a sudden he kicked this big metal cabinet with his wooden leg. It sounded like a hand grenade had gone off. He scared the hell out of us.

Considering all the commotion, we got out of there and back to our hotel as quickly as we could. The next morning, Lee MacPhail, the league president, called to ask me what had happened. I told him there was no excuse for what happened and I thought the White Sox should be held accountable. MacPhail agreed and declared the game a forfeit, giving the victory to Detroit.

It really was an absolute fiasco. Veeck was noted for his promotions and his marketing ability, but this night was not one of his most happy, creative, successful ideas. Thirty-seven people were arrested, and I was surprised there weren't any serious injuries. Luckily, nobody has ever tried to stage a promotion of that sort again.

It had been five years earlier, in 1974, that another terrible idea touched off a near riot at a game in Cleveland. Fortunately, I wasn't there, but everybody heard about it. As a means to increase attendance for a game against Texas, the Indians sold beer that night for 10 cents a cup. The Indians were trailing by two runs in the bottom of the ninth, but they rallied to tie the game. Despite the fact that there were only two outs, hundreds of fans poured onto the field. By that time, the fans were so drunk they couldn't count to three. They attempted to throw beer on the players and umpires, and when one zealous fan tried to make Rangers outfielder Jeff Burroughs give him his glove, Burroughs threatened the fan with his bat.

Officials later determined that the crowd of about twenty-five thousand people had consumed about sixty thousand 10-ounce beers. The Indians were forced to forfeit the game to the Rangers. Luckily, Major League Baseball finally realized that promotions like that are unsafe and ridiculous and that the best promotion is to have a winning team.

Other than Veeck, probably the most innovative owner during my years in the majors was Oakland's Charlie Finley. He was always having hot-pants day or something like that, and he was the first owner to introduce ballgirls, dressing attractive young ladies in skimpy outfits and positioning them down the left-field and right-field lines to retrieve foul balls. One of the people who held that job was Debbie Fields. You might recognize her better now as Mrs. Fields, of the cookie company of the same name.

Charlie was the only reason the umpires wore red coats for a few years, because he thought we were too dull and the game needed more color to be more exciting. He introduced all of the multiple-colored uniforms and the different hats for road and home games. He had his manager and coaches wear white hats while the players wore green. He also had his players wear white shoes instead of the traditional black, and he introduced the orange baseball. I worked a game in spring training with the orange baseballs, but that never caught on. He encouraged his players to grow mustaches and even tried to talk Vida Blue into changing his name to True Blue.

One of the young boys who used to take care of our dressing room in Oakland was nicknamed Hammer, because he looked exactly like Hank Aaron. When Finley went through one of his purges of employees, he moved Hammer up to be his executive vice president. He later went on to become a pretty good rap music star using the same name.

Finley had many disputes with Bowie Kuhn, who was the commissioner at the time. When Finley didn't like the direction baseball was headed, he sold the A's and got out. In many ways he was ahead of his time as an owner, and he got out when he recognized how money was going to change the game. He made the right decision.

We have been lucky that umpires, and the players and coaches for that matter, have very seldom been attacked by drunk or crazed fans. I was working the playoffs in 1981 at Yankee Stadium when a fan ran out and tackled umpire Mike Reilly, who was working third base. There was no reason for the attack, but I guess the guy was drunk and somebody probably bet or dared him to do it. Yankee Stadium always has been one of the scarier places to work over the years. But New York's finest always make unruly guests wish they had been better behaved.

We had two problems recently in Chicago at Comiskey Park, when two fans came out and attacked Royals coach Tom Gamboa, and then in a separate incident when a fan came on the field and tackled umpire Laz Diaz. Our court system needs to make the penalties much more severe for actions like that, including possible jail time, because someday somebody will be injured badly.

One of the worst incidents I was involved in during my career came not on the field but at a hotel in Detroit. Our crew had flown in from Oakland, and sitting in first class, we had all the free drinks we wanted. I probably had a few more than I needed, and I wasn't feeling well when we reached the hotel.

I checked in, got the key to my room, and asked the bellhop to bring up my bags. When I got to the room, the door was open slightly and the bed was made. I set my wallet and other personal items out on the dresser and lay down sideways across the bed, with a headache, to wait for the bellhop.

Of course I fell asleep, and I didn't wake up until several hours later. It took me a little while, but once I was awake enough to figure out where I was, I realized everything had been taken out of my wallet and was lying around the room. My suitcases were also missing.

I picked up the phone and called the front desk and said, "Where are my bags?" The clerk asked who I was and when I said Dave Phillips, she said they were in my room. "I'm in my room and they aren't here," I said. She asked what room I was in, and when I said 503 or whatever number was on the phone, she said, "No, you're supposed to be in 609."

They brought me up a new key, and sure enough my bags were in the other room. Somehow my room had been switched, and they had not given me the right key. The bellhop or somebody had realized I was asleep, in the wrong room, and went through my wallet and took the $40 or $50 in cash I had on me. Luckily he didn't take my credit cards or any of my other belongings.

Fortunately for me, almost every other incident I've been involved with has happened on the field. Many of them were quite memorable.

4

Spitballs and
Illegal Substances

Gaylord Perry had been pitching in the major leagues for
nine seasons when I broke into the majors, but he was
in the National League, fooling hitters with his spitball or
greaseball with the San Francisco Giants. My luck, and that
of every other A.L. umpire, changed when he was traded to
Cleveland before the 1972 season.

I was working with a new crew for that season, headed
by Nestor Chylak. He is one of eight umpires in the Hall of
Fame, but at that point in his career I think he was past his
prime. He was very egotistical and extremely competitive,
especially with his own crew. By the time I began working
with him, he was starting to have some difficulty behind the
plate. None of the managers and few players would say anything to him, however, because he had earned a reputation
as a good umpire.

A good reputation is perhaps the most important intangible an umpire can possess. The hardest part about it is, you have to earn it. There is no other way to get it. You can't walk into Kmart and buy credibility. If you could, every new umpire would be standing in line when the store opened.

Until you earn that status, managers and players are going to challenge you all the time. They are going to scream and yell at you. They are going to call you every name in the book, just to find out if you can take it and see how you are going to respond. It's all about intimidation.

Because of his experience, Nestor had earned and deserved that status. Still, I had a hard time believing what happened when we opened the season in Cleveland. Nestor was behind the plate, Perry was pitching his first game ever in the A.L., and I was working second base. The start of the season had been delayed for six days because of a players strike.

Nestor appeared to be having a difficult day. I was looking straight in from second base, and I couldn't believe it. I could see Perry was really getting upset and was staring in at Nestor as if to say, "Where was that pitch?" I knew the other two guys on our crew—Jim Evans and Larry Barnett—did not have the proper view to see the pitches, but they also knew Perry was questioning Nestor's calls.

Perry had a reputation for throwing a spitball, which is an illegal pitch. I don't know if Nestor had trouble calling the pitches because they were spitballs, but the four of us went to dinner that night and Nestor was bragging about how he had really shown Perry who was the boss and how that pitcher was never going to fool with him. In other words, he was embarrassed that he had a mediocre game and he was making excuses.

I should have known then that it was going to be a difficult year. It was a difficult year for baseball itself as well. It was the only time in the history of baseball that a pennant was decided by a half game. Instead of figuring out how to make up the games postponed by the strike so that everybody would play the same number of games and a full season, baseball's leaders, without any foresight or thought, decided to just begin the season six days late. That meant that Detroit played 156 games and the Red Sox 155, and Detroit won the A.L. East by half a game with an 86–70 record, compared to Boston's 85–70 record. It was an absolute joke and a disgrace for Major League Baseball.

After opening the year in Cleveland we went to Baltimore for a series between the Tigers and the Orioles, Billy Martin against Earl Weaver. I had the plate for the first game. There was a big headline in the newspaper quoting Martin about what a crucial series this was going to be, how it would set the tone for the season. Hell, it was only the third game of the season and he was saying how crucial it was. The Orioles had lost the World Series the previous year, and this really had the atmosphere of a playoff series.

Because it was my first game of the season behind the plate, and because I was with a new crew chief, I was probably a little nervous. Joe Coleman was pitching for Detroit, and he always thought that if *he* threw the ball, it was a strike. About the third inning, he started staring in at me and questioning my judgment. I headed for the mound for a confrontation—something that Nestor couldn't or wouldn't do two days earlier. Martin got there about the same time, and I ejected him right away. I almost ran Coleman and Bill Freehan, the catcher, too, but Martin took over the argument to make sure he was the only one ejected. Chylak, my crew chief, never came in to help me, and my friends Barnett and Evans were too young to help.

We finished the game, and it was a tough game to work. Afterward, we were in the dressing room and Nestor was sitting in front of his locker, smoking a cigarette, shaking his head. His shoulders were hunched over, and he was staring at the floor just mumbling to himself. "Major league umpire my ass," I heard him say. Dick Butler, the supervisor, had encouraged the young umpires to ask Nestor after games if he had seen anything that we could do better. Unfortunately, I asked the question, and he immediately started screaming at me.

"Did I see anything?" he yelled. "You were a good umpire last year." He just sat there shaking his head. I was absolutely devastated. I had had a tough game, and now I was dreading the next 150 games I would have to work with this jerk.

Chylak, Evans, and Barnett were going out for a drink that night, but there was no way I was going with them. I had had enough of Chylak. I went back to my hotel room in a depressed state of mind, because of his comments.

About 2:00 A.M., there was a knock on my door. It was Barnett. Along with Evans, Larry is one of my closest friends in the world to this day. We were in each other's weddings (and, coincidentally, we both married women named Sharon).

Larry said, "Are you all right?" I said I was OK. Larry was concerned because he knew Chylak had hurt my feelings. Larry said, "You think that was bad? That wasn't even close to being a tough game. I had games like that almost every day my first year. I would get so upset that I would be sitting there watching television and wouldn't even realize the TV channel had been off for hours. There was just snow on the screen."

That thoughtful visit from Larry taught me a valuable lesson that I've never forgotten. When a young umpire has a bad day, he always thinks he is the only one who has ever experienced something like that. The greatest thing a veteran umpire can give to a young umpire is to let him know he has had similar situations. It does help your confidence when you realize that other umpires have had tough days too. Chylak obviously didn't believe in building up our confidence. On the contrary—he enjoyed seeing us struggle.

The next year, Larry had a game, working with me and another older umpire, Frank Umont. It was after a doubleheader, and Frank wasn't thinking about anything except where he could get a drink. Larry worked the plate, and afterward he asked if Frank, the crew chief, had seen anything that he had done wrong, and it took Umont about five minutes to answer.

His sarcastic answer was, "You know, kid, you must have done something wrong because all they did was f****** yell at you all day long."

You could have stabbed Larry with a knife and it would not have cut so deep. What a crew chief should have said in that situation was something to the effect that "it was a tough game; there were a lot of tough pitches." Be positive and create confidence. That's what a young umpire needs. Chylak and Umont must have missed that lesson at umpire's school.

Larry left soon after that when his wife was having a baby, and he told Dick Butler to put him with another crew when he came back so he wouldn't ever have to work with Umont again. Unfortunately, I had to stay with him for another month.

There were a lot of umpires who had trouble with particular players, and despite Gaylord Perry's reputation, I never had a serious problem with him until 1982, when he was pitching with Seattle.

Umpires always hated it when Perry was pitching because there was always a possibility there would be problems. You knew it was going to be a long game, because batters were going to ask you to check the baseball, and even if he wasn't throwing a spitter, he was going to go through all the motions and shenanigans to make the hitters think he was throwing the spitter. It definitely was a mental game that he created.

On this night, the Mariners were playing the Red Sox, and I happened to have the plate. Our crew was exhausted because we had traveled all day to get to Seattle, and I remember that I had not shaved when I went to the stadium.

It was a typical Perry game, with the hitters asking me to look at the ball almost every inning. When Boston came to bat in the fifth inning, the leadoff batter, Reid Nichols, asked me to check the ball while Perry was warming up.

I thought that was a little unusual, but I decided I might as well do it then so perhaps I wouldn't have to stop again later in the inning. After about the fifth warm-up pitch I asked Jim Essian, the catcher, to let me see the ball, and he flipped it to me.

I was giving it the quick once-over, when all of a sudden I noticed my fingerprint appear on the ball. I could see my fingerprint in grease. I looked at the ball again, almost in shock that it was so visible, and then I looked at Perry. He was standing there, kind of annoyed, waiting for me to throw him the ball.

As soon as Perry made eye contact with me, it was like the guy who knew he had cheated and had just been caught. I started to walk to the mound, and when I got about halfway there, he threw his arms up in the air and yelled, "I didn't put anything on the ball." I had not even said a word to him yet.

I got to the mound about the same time the Seattle manager, Rene Lachemann, got there. Because it had been a warm-up pitch, I could not say he had thrown an illegal pitch. If that had happened on an official pitch I could have ejected him immediately.

I said, "I don't know how this grease got here," pointing to the grease on the ball. "But it's here, and consider this your warning. If anything appears at any other time during the game, or I deem you have thrown an illegal pitch, you will be ejected." They were both happy and relieved, because it was like a state trooper letting you off with a warning instead of giving you a speeding ticket.

There wasn't really anything Perry or Lachemann could say back to me, because they could see the grease too, and we continued the game. Two innings later, there were two outs with runners on first and third, and Rick Miller was coming up to bat. Lachemann came out of the dugout, and I breathed a sigh of relief, because I knew Perry was going to be taken out of the game. I even took out my lineup card and circled his name because I was sure he was going to be replaced.

However, when I looked up, Lachemann was gone and Perry was still out there. I know Perry, who was older than

Lachemann, talked him out of taking him out of the game by assuring Lachemann that he could get Miller out.

The first pitch was a ball, but then Perry threw his number one pitch, the spitter. If you can imagine how a ball rolls across the table and then gets to the edge and falls straight down, that's exactly what this pitch did. It looked like it was about an 88-mph fastball, and about the time Miller started to swing, the ball dropped straight to the ground. It was clearly an illegal pitch, and I had no doubt in my mind Perry would be ejected.

Later, watching the play on videotape, I could see my hands motion time had been called just as Miller was looking back at me, no doubt to complain about what he knew was a spitter. I walked in front of the plate and yelled to Perry, "That's it. You're gone."

Despite all of the allegations and suspicions, it was the first time in Perry's 21 years in the major leagues he had been ejected. Perry had a lot to say later, but he didn't say anything then. He was embarrassed and looked like a deer in headlights.

The fans at the Kingdome let me know how they felt. It happened to be cushion night, and the fans displayed their anger by giving me their cushions. They were there only because of Perry, but I knew I was right. There was absolutely no doubt in my mind.

The crowd of about twenty thousand people was furious at me, but it never bothered me because nobody ever told me I would be popular when I became an umpire.

I always walk back to the screen in between innings, and the fans were really blasting me. The seats at the Kingdome were about 12 to 15 feet above the playing field, but I stood there thinking it would be possible for somebody to jump over the railing and attack me, if they really wanted to.

About that time, I felt a tap on my shoulder. It scared me and I jumped. I'm jumpy anyway, but even more so than normal in that situation. I turned around, expecting to see a fan ready to kick my ass, but it was Randy Adamack, the Mariners' public relations director. He scared the hell out of me. I think he could tell I was a little spooked, and he apologized, but he said he needed to ask if I would come to a press conference after the game. That was when I remembered I had not shaved. I looked pretty tired and grungy at that news conference.

Perry was suspended for 10 days and fined. When you consider how many games he pitched throwing that spitball, and how successful he was—earning election to the Hall of Fame—I suspect he would say the penalty was worth it. Today he jokes about that game and about using illegal pitches.

When people hear about a guy throwing a spitball, they might think he can do it just by putting a little spit on his hand or grease on his finger. It is not nearly that simple. Perry had really mastered the pitch and learned how to throw it. A lot of veteran pitchers, I think, try to learn how to throw it later in their careers if they think it will help them stay in the big leagues for a few extra years. What they learn, however, is that it is not an easy pitch to throw. Bob Forsch, the Cardinals' veteran pitcher, late in his career told me he tried to throw a grease ball but couldn't control it and actually threw it against the screen. A lot of other pitchers had the same problem.

Perry had a lot of places on his body where he could hide the stuff. When you walked out to him on the mound, it was like walking into your son's or daughter's room when they had a cold and their mom had Vicks rubbed all over their chest. That's the way he smelled on the mound. Your eyes always got kind of watery when you got near him because he had so much Vicks on him. It could be 30 degrees outside and his uniform would be totally soaked from sweat because of all the stuff he had on him. Gaylord would have put 10W-30 oil on his uniform if he could find a way to do it. He didn't care, as long as he could throw the spitter.

One guy who readily admitted to me that he threw a spitball when he pitched in the majors was Bill Kunkel, who later became an umpire. He pitched in the A.L. from 1961 to 1963, and he said, "Without it, do you think I would have spent three years in the majors?"

I was working with Kunkel and Jim Evans in 1975, and Kunkel invited us to his house for a barbecue after a day game in New York. Evans was laughing and kidding him about throwing a spitball, and I don't think he truly believed Bill, so he challenged him to throw one.

Kunkel was still a pretty good athlete, and he stepped off where the mound should be, and Evans got down to catch him. After a couple of warm-up pitches, Evans said, "OK, load one up. Let's see your best stuff."

Kunkel loaded one up and let it go. Evans tried to catch it, but the bottom dropped out of it and the ball hit him right in the knee. Of course he wasn't wearing any catching gear. Jim was screaming in pain, and Kunkel and I were doubled over because we were laughing so hard.

Every spitball is just a little bit different, kind of like a knuckleball. I guess it has to do with the arm speed, the amount of stuff you put on the ball, and where you put it. Even though it is called a spitball, I think most of the time a pitcher uses K-Y jelly, Vaseline, or, in Perry's case, Vicks. Some guys use soap—anything slick that can be rubbed on a uniform and not be seen will work, if they can get away with it.

Other pitchers have tried different ways to throw illegal pitches over the years, and another one I happened to catch in the act was Joe Niekro.

The game was in 1987, when Niekro was pitching for the Minnesota Twins. We were in Anaheim, and Gene Mauch was managing the Angels. He had Don Sutton pitching on his team, and there had been some suggestions over the years that Sutton also threw some illegal pitches, so I am sure Mauch was not going to go out of his way to complain about Niekro.

A rookie umpire, Tim Tschida, was working the plate, and I was at first base. Tschida walked up to me between innings and said a few of the California hitters were complaining that Niekro was scuffing the ball. He showed me a couple of balls that he had confiscated. Sure enough, they were scuffed in the exact same spot, over the league president's signature.

I told Tim, "Put them back in your pocket and make sure you know where they are. I will check some balls at the end of the inning. I will get the other guys to be on the lookout as well."

I found two that were scuffed in the same spot, and Steve Palermo did as well. Tim came down to me again, and I told him that if he saw another pitch that he thought was illegal, we were going to go to the mound to check Joe out. I told him just to nod to me and I would be right there with him.

Tim didn't even need to nod. I saw the pitch, and we both headed for the mound. Niekro was standing there with an expression like, "What do you want?" I said, "We've got several balls that are all scuffed in the same spot and we noticed that you keep going to your back pocket."

By this time, Tom Kelly, the manager of the Twins, and the catcher, Sal Butera, were at the mound as well. After we asked to see what he had in his back pocket, Joe reached into it and slowly pulled out a baseball card. "What's this?" I said.

"It's a baseball card of my son," Niekro said. "I always carry it when I pitch. Is this what you were looking for?"

I smiled and said, "No, that isn't what I had in mind." He had a little grin on his face. "What else do you have back there?" I said.

He put both of his hands in the pockets—that became a somewhat famous picture—and pulled the pockets inside out at the same time. As he did this, I saw a little flash of something come out and fall to the ground, right by my feet. Palermo was standing right next to me, and he saw it too. Out of the corner of my eye I saw Steve had this strange look on his face.

I reached down and picked it up. It was a broken piece of emery board. "What's this?" I asked Niekro. He said, trying to sound very innocent, "Oh, I use that to file my nails in between innings."

I didn't believe him for a minute, and it didn't really matter because it was illegal to carry that while pitching, so he was automatically ejected. I found out later Niekro and the catcher, Butera, had a plan in the event he was ever searched on the mound. Butera was supposed to stand behind him, and when Niekro emptied his pockets and flipped the emery board into the air, he was supposed to catch it and hide it in his glove, but Sal missed it.

We collected five or six of the scuffed baseballs, and I gave them to one of the batboys and told him to put them in my locker. As the kid was taking them to the dressing room, one of the Twins players, Al Newman, who now is their third-base coach, tackled the kid, wrestled him to the ground, and took the baseballs. He thought he was contributing to the team.

The kid ran out and told Tschida what happened, and Tim told me. I immediately called Kelly out of the dugout. I really like Tom and always thought he did a great job all of those years he managed the Twins. He always impressed me as someone with great integrity, who was fair and a true professional. I explained the problem.

He looked me directly in the eye and said, "Dave, I promise you those balls will be in your dressing room when this game is over. I apologize. I will take care of it."

I said, "Tom, I know you will handle this. Thank you." The batboy almost had tears in his eyes because he felt so bad about what happened, but it was not his fault. He was trying to do his job.

After the game, as promised, the balls were in our dressing room. Kelly was a leader and ran his team with an iron fist, and I knew he would do the right thing.

I also was impressed with the way Tom managed Jack Morris, who came over to the Twins late in his career. Morris was one of the most difficult players to work with in the major leagues. He was always bitching about something. He was a good pitcher and a good competitor, but he was never happy about anything. When Morris pitched for the Tigers, Sparky Anderson, a great manager, let him get away with acting that way, I suspect because he was their star pitcher. When Morris pitched for Kelly, however, he never bothered anybody. Kelly never allowed his players to act in an unprofessional manner. He would not tolerate it.

One night I was working third base, and Morris was pitching. Mike Pagliarulo was playing third for the Twins, and something had happened—I don't remember if it was an error or some other close play. I said to Mike, "You better not make an error behind this guy because he will start screaming at you." Pagliarulo was a blue-collar player and a good guy. He looked at me and said, "I want to tell you something, Davey. If Jack ever screams at me about missing a ball or anything else, I will kick his ass right on that mound. He had better never yell at me."

I couldn't help but laugh. I started rooting for Mike to make an error so that Morris would scream at Mike and Mike could beat the hell out of him. I would have truly loved to have seen Jack get his ass kicked on the mound.

Niekro was suspended for 10 days for scuffing the ball, but he came back and pitched in the World Series that year as the Twins beat the Cardinals. He actually had some fun with the suspension and publicity. He went on the *Tonight Show* wearing a full carpenter's tool belt with a sander and all kinds of tools. He really had no defense, so it was a credit to him that he had fun with it.

Joe was kind of a unique case. I don't believe he threw illegal pitches throughout his whole career, like Perry did.

Because he was a knuckleball pitcher, Joe knew he had to develop a pitch other than his 82-mph fastball that he could use when he fell behind in the count. He also was not the pitcher his brother, Phil, was. Phil just threw knuckleballs his whole career and had great success with it.

Don Sutton was suspected of throwing illegal pitches, especially late in his career. One night we were working in Anaheim, and the other team asked us to check his glove. When Doug Harvey, a National League umpire, tried to check him in Dodger Stadium, he walked off the mound and threatened to call his lawyer. When he tried to threaten us like that, I said, "Either you let us check you or you will be ejected."

He let us look at his glove, but I had the feeling when he handed me his glove I would not find anything wrong or he would not have given it up so easily. It was clean, but that didn't erase the suspicions teams had of him. Still, I always liked and respected Don and thought he was a true professional and a very good pitcher.

Like a spitball, a knuckleball is a hard pitch for an umpire to call because it can break all over the place. It usually does not come to the plate in one pattern. The best knuckleball pitcher I ever worked as far as consistency was concerned was Wilbur Wood. He had a great ability to throw it for strikes, and he always pitched quickly. I loved to work his games.

One thing I learned about pitchers is that some were so naïve they really didn't even know they were doing anything wrong, unlike guys like Perry, who was very determined and well aware of what he was doing. A pitcher who fell into the innocent category was Grant Jackson, who pitched for many teams.

When Jackson was with Kansas City, he came into a game in relief, and I was working first base. When he crossed my path, he very casually said to me, "Hey, Dave, can I pitch with this Band-Aid on my finger?"

He was very sincere as he walked over and showed me his hand. I saw the Band-Aid, but I also saw something else. His palm and fingers were covered in pine tar.

"Well, the Band-Aid doesn't really bother me, but what is this stuff all over your hand?" I asked.

Very matter-of-factly, Jackson said, "Oh, that's pine tar. I use it because it helps me get a better grip on my curveball."

He was so open about it, I knew he felt there was nothing wrong with what he was doing. A batter is allowed to use pine tar to get a better grip on his bat, so it seemed logical to Jackson that he ought to be able to use pine tar as a pitcher.

"I hate to disappoint you," I said, "but you can't pitch with pine tar on your hand. That's illegal."

He was almost dumbfounded, insisting that he had to use it or he couldn't throw his curveball. We made him get a towel and wipe it off.

Pitchers, of course, are not the only players who have been known to cheat if they thought they could get away with it. Many hitters have been just as guilty.

5

Pine Tar and Corked Bats

When you think of all the great hitters who have played for the Yankees over the years, the name Graig Nettles isn't the first one that comes up. In 1974, however, Nettles got off to an amazing start.

The Yankees were playing their first of two seasons at Shea Stadium, the Mets' home, because their stadium was being renovated. Nettles, the third baseman, set an American League record by hitting 11 home runs in the month of April. (That mark has since been broken by Ken Griffey Jr., who hit 13 for the Mariners in April 1997.)

I don't think anybody suspected Nettles of doing anything illegal. He was a great third baseman and likely would have won several Gold Gloves if he didn't happen to play in the same era as Brooks Robinson. He also was a very good hitter, having hit 22 or more homers in three of his four previous seasons. As far as I know there were never any allegations, during that season or any previous year, that he was using a corked bat.

The Yankees were playing the Tigers in the second game of a doubleheader on September 7, and I was working third base. Nettles was batting in the fifth inning, and he hit a ball that made me flinch. I thought the ball was coming directly at me. When I looked up, however, I saw the ball had gone into left field. What had been headed toward me was a section of his bat, which had split in two.

When I walked over to pick it up, I saw it was a six- to eight-inch section of the bat, perfectly sawed off. That is not the normal way a bat breaks. I looked a little closer, and I could see the cork. Someone had sawed the bat, drilled a hole and filled it with cork, and then glued the bat back together with Krazy Glue. It really was unbelievable to think it would work, but it had until that point in the season. He had probably hit the ball off the end of the bat, and that put just enough stress on the bat to pop that piece off. The Tigers were upset, naturally, because Nettles had no doubt used the same bat when he hit a home run in the second inning, but there wasn't anything we could do about that. It turned out that was the only run of the game, and the Yankees won 1–0.

Nettles was called out. He maintained it was the first time he had used the bat, which he said was given to him for good luck by a fan in Chicago. He honestly said that with a straight face.

It wasn't the first time, of course, that a hitter had used a corked bat, and it certainly won't be the last. Just last year, in 2003, Sammy Sosa of the Cubs was caught using a corked bat and was suspended. It was really a shame because I always liked Sammy and we had a very good relationship when he first came up with the Texas Rangers.

Sammy was striking out a lot with the Rangers, but I really liked his personality. He was traded to the White Sox and still was striking out too much, but you could see he was the kind of player who really wanted to improve. General manager Larry Himes had brought Sammy to the White Sox, and when he left to become the general manager of the Cubs, he brought Sammy over there with him.

It was with the Cubs that Sammy's career really blossomed, as he became a big home-run hitter and captivated the fans, especially with his battle against the Cardinals' Mark McGwire for the home-run crown in 1998. I always thought he was a good athlete, but he never impressed me as the kind of hitter who would hit 60 homers in a season or 500 for his career. He was a player that definitely was good for the game. His home-run race with McGwire came at a critical time for baseball as it desperately tried to rebound from the disastrous strike in 1994.

The problem with Sammy getting caught using a corked bat, of course, is that it taints all of his accomplishments. He said the bat in question was supposed to be used only for batting practice and home-run contests, but even that is wrong. I honestly don't believe it was the only corked bat he had in his collection.

Baseball was really concerned about its image. In my opinion, it was amazing how quickly the executives moved past the incident and accepted Sammy's excuse. It seemed as if they wanted to substantiate his story that it was just a one-time mistake. I think they realized the marketing ability of

Sammy was still immense, and I think they were scared the fallout would be worse than it was.

What is amazing to me is that it has never been proven to my knowledge how a corked bat helps you hit the ball farther. Everybody I've talked to and everything I've read from the scientific studies say nobody can tell if it helps or not. The only advantage I can see is that it takes an ounce or two out of the weight of the bat, making it lighter, which gives a hitter better bat speed as he swings it through the zone. But I think the biggest impact of corking a bat is psychological. If a hitter thinks he is going to be able to hit the ball harder or farther because he is using a corked bat, he just might be able to do it. The bottom line is that it is illegal, and for Sammy to simply say he used it when he wanted to put on a show is wrong. I don't think he has been using a corked bat his entire career, but there will no doubt be some skeptics who will believe he has.

Another hitter who had a little problem with a corked bat in my presence was Albert Belle, when he was playing for Cleveland in 1994.

Although he had a terrible image with the media and many fans, I always liked Belle. He went by the name Joey when he first came to the major leagues, but for some reason he changed his name to Albert. To me Joey always sounded more like a baseball player. He was portrayed as a tough guy, but he was always good with the umpires. He didn't bother anybody to speak of, and he struck me as an intelligent guy. He was a very focused player and played the game hard.

The Indians were playing the White Sox in Chicago on July 15, 1994. I was working the plate. Sometimes when a team is going to challenge something about a player or a game, they will give the umpires a heads-up about what they are planning to do. But when Gene Lamont, the manager of the White Sox, approached me when Belle came to bat in the first inning, I had no idea what was on his mind.

Lamont asked me to check Belle's bat, saying he believed it was illegal. If an umpire is asked to check a bat, he is obligated to do so and remove that bat from the game. If the umpire finds anything suspicious about the bat, he can eject the player on the spot.

After Lamont made his request, I told Belle I needed to check his bat. He handed it to me, and I looked at it. I scratched the top of it and inspected the bat thoroughly, but I did not see anything that looked as if it had been tampered with. It was a black bat with a white handle, but I could not detect any tampering.

For Lamont to make that request, he must have been acting on some information that he received, which led him to believe the bat had been corked. When the Indians arrived in Chicago the previous night, I suspect someone had x-rayed Belle's bat and they thought the x-rays showed it was corked.

I took the bat and gave it to our clubhouse attendant, Vinny Fresso, and asked him to put it in my locker. Belle got a different bat, we went on with the game, and I kind of forgot about it—until I was walking toward our dressing room after the game.

As I reached the corridor to our dressing room, I noticed there was a big entourage of people outside the door. I knew most of them, and I couldn't figure out why they were there. Ron Schueler, the general manager of the White Sox, was there, as was Phyllis Merhige of the A.L. office. I didn't even know she was in town. They were all executive-type people; none of them were media.

Ron had been a pitcher and then a scout with the A's, and I knew him well. He approached me first and said, "Dave, we've got a big problem." I was surprised. The game was over and it went without incident, so I didn't understand what the big problem was. "We've had a break-in of your dressing room," he said.

I walked into the room, and they all followed me. Ron was talking, but I wasn't listening to what he was saying. I was thinking about all of the things I was concerned had been stolen—my Rolex watch, my World Series ring, cash. Ron was saying, "Can you identify the bat?" but it was just going over my head as I thought about what I had brought with me to the game that day.

As I looked into my locker, I saw that all of my personal items were still there, including some that I had left out in plain sight. My watch, my rings, the cash in my wallet—none of it had been touched. I turned back to Ron, very confused about what was going on. He said again, "Can you identify the bat?" This time I heard him.

Ron pointed to a section of the ceiling, and I could tell one of the bars holding up the drop ceiling had been badly bent. Someone had apparently crawled through the crawl space above the ceiling and dropped into our dressing room. Vinny had discovered the break-in near the end of the game, when he had gone back into the room to get it ready for the umpires after the game.

"What do you mean can I identify the bat?" I asked Ron. With that, they rolled out an extremely large picture on the table, taken in the first inning, of me looking at Belle's bat. "Is the bat in your locker the same bat as the one in this picture?" Ron said.

It took me about two seconds to answer that no, it was not Belle's bat.

"You would testify to that?" Ron said, and I said sure. It did not take a Rhodes scholar to tell it was not the same bat.

It then became obvious to me what had happened. Whoever had broken in had switched the bats. The one in the locker was the same color, black with a white handle, but you could tell it was in terrible condition and had been used quite frequently. It turned out to be Paul Sorrento's bat. They could not switch it with another Belle bat because all of his bats must have been corked.

The office of the groundskeeper at the park is adjacent to the umpires' dressing room, and he told team officials that he was taking a nap sitting in his chair during the game when he felt something hit his face. He realized it was some insulation from the drop ceiling—the culprit had apparently thought he was over our dressing room when he really was over that office.

I was asked not to mention anything about the incident to the press, and I agreed to stay quiet unless a reporter asked me about it. I told Schueler I would not lie.

I really was about to brush the whole thing off and not treat it like a big deal, until I got back to the hotel. Sharon had come up from St. Louis for the series, and when I told her about it, she was really shocked. She asked, "Doesn't baseball have a security guy? You ought to call him because that is a crime."

After I slept on it, I decided Sharon was right. There was nothing about the break-in in either Chicago newspaper the next morning, only reports that we had confiscated Belle's bat. I called Bobby Brown, the president of the American League. He didn't seem very interested and just asked me to send in a report. I then called Kevin Hallinan, baseball's head of security, and left a message with his wife. Kevin called back 30 minutes later.

"I guess you heard about what happened here last night?" I asked Kevin, assuming the answer would be yes. He told me he had no idea what I was talking about. "You're kidding me," he responded. I told him the whole story, and I could tell he was taking the incident very seriously. "Dave, I will be in Chicago this afternoon, and I will meet you at the ballpark," he said.

When our crew got to Comiskey Park about 4:00 P.M., the entire area around our dressing room was blocked off with the yellow tape the police use at a crime scene. There were six or seven Chicago police officers there, and some were crawling in the roof and testing for fingerprints. Kevin was there, and he said he would talk with me after the game. I thought maybe the police had found out what happened. Kevin asked if I could meet him in the morning, and when we met, he brought a bat and asked me if it was Belle's bat. It wasn't. He said OK and told me to meet him at the stadium.

When I got to the meeting, Kevin was there, along with John Hart, the GM of the Indians; Ron Schueler; Jerry Reinsdorf, the owner of the White Sox; and both managers, Gene Lamont and Mike Hargrove. By this time, the Indians had finally come clean and given Kevin the bat. He asked me if I could identify it and I said, "That's it."

Now that we had the bat, the question was who had taken it. It was obvious why they had taken it—the Indians were in the middle of a pennant race and didn't want to lose their best hitter to a 10-game suspension. There was speculation that the suspect was a front-office employee of the Indians, but that was never proven. Over the years, another name gradually surfaced—that of a pitcher with the Indians, Jason Grimsley.

I didn't know for sure, but I thought it was Grimsley. A few years later, I was working the plate in a game in Anaheim, and Grimsley was there with his new team. I went over to the dugout in between innings to get a drink of water and put a towel on my head, and Grimsley struck up a casual conversation with me about how hot it was.

When I realized it was him, I very casually said back, "So, you been stealing any bats lately?" The smile disappeared from his face, but he knew he had been caught. "How did you know it was me?" he said, confirming my belief.

I really didn't know. I was just curious to see if he would admit it, and he did. It turns out he had crawled 100 feet through the crawl space from the Indians locker room to the umpires' dressing room, then dropped down, switched the bats, and crawled back. To my knowledge he was never fined or suspended for his actions.

When Belle's bat was finally cut open, it was found to be corked. He was suspended for 10 games and fined, although the suspension was later reduced to 7 games.

Belle left Cleveland to play for the White Sox and later moved on to Baltimore. I predicted when he joined the Orioles that he would be the guy to break Roger Maris' record of 61 homers in a season, and I think he might have had a chance if he had not been beset by injuries.

A lot of sportswriters and fans rave about Camden Yards, the new stadium in Baltimore, and it is a beautiful stadium in a terrific location. It is a great people-watching park and a great park to watch a game. From the standpoint of an umpire or a pitcher, however, it is a terrible park. There are no outs in the stadium because there is so little foul territory. If a hitter doesn't hit the ball fair, he keeps hitting. I told the Orioles' manager they ought to just move the batting cage behind home plate and leave it there.

I was working a game there one night when Alex Fernandez was pitching for the White Sox, and he was nearly unhittable. He took a no-hitter deep into the game, and I really thought he was going to get it. Then Roberto Alomar came up to bat. He reached out to try to protect the plate and hit what looked like a routine fly ball, but it kept drifting and drifting, and before you knew it, it was a home run. It was ball movement like that at Camden yards that made me think Belle had a real chance to break Maris' record, but unfortunately he could not stay healthy.

While everyone in baseball knows about corked bats, there is another way hitters can doctor their bats—by putting too much pine tar on them. If it has never been proven that a corked bat can make a ball go farther, I sure as heck know it can't be proven that putting too much pine tar on a bat can affect the distance a ball is hit.

You wouldn't be able to tell that to some managers, however.

The Royals, managed by Whitey Herzog, were playing the Angels once, and Bill Kunkel was working the plate. I was at first. One thing about Kunkel was that he always tried to defuse any argument he had by acting like it was about something else. That was what happened this day, and it got him in the middle of a gigantic mess.

Dave Chalk led off an inning for the Angels. Kunkel called a strike and Chalk didn't agree with the call. He stepped out and looked back at Kunkel. On the next pitch, the same thing happened. Kunkel never wanted people to think Chalk or anyone else was questioning his strike calls, so he reached out and asked Chalk for his bat. He laid it down on the plate and measured it to see if it had too much pine tar, which was his way of showing the fans and media that Chalk wasn't arguing with him about balls and strikes.

The batboy brought out a towel, and they wiped the bat off a little bit. The game went on, and John Mayberry hit two home runs. I had gone down the right-field line to watch the ball on his second homer, and when I turned around and started back to the infield, I saw Dick Williams, the Angels' manager, standing at home plate. He looked like he was there to congratulate Mayberry, which I knew wasn't the reason he was there—not the Williams I knew.

What he was doing was challenging Mayberry's bat, saying it had too much pine tar on it. Kunkel had created this mess by checking Chalk's bat, and I knew he was going to have a tough time getting out of it.

Kunkel took the bat and measured it, and even though it appeared a little over the limit, Kunkel said it was OK. Williams said he was protesting the game.

When I got to the dressing room after the game, Red Patterson, an executive with the Angels, was waiting. He said, "Lee MacPhail's going to be calling in a little while."

Kunkel didn't show up for quite a while, and it turned out he was in Herzog's office. Whitey was telling him, "I never told you to check Chalk's bat. Don't bring me into this."

Finally Kunkel came into the room. There was a knock on the door, and it was none other than Dick Williams. "I'm supposed to come over here for a phone call," he said. I let him in, and sure enough the phone rang. I happened to be the closest to it, so I answered it. It was Lee MacPhail. He asked to speak to Bill.

I never could stand Dick Williams, so I was kind of getting a kick out of watching him get madder and madder as Bill talked to Lee about everything except what he was calling about. Bill was asking about the fishing in New Jersey—anything he could think of to ignore the real reason MacPhail was calling. Finally I could tell that Lee had asked him about Mayberry's bat and the pine tar. After all the B.S. he had to make the crucial comment.

"I measured it and it was within legal limits," Kunkel said into the phone.

When he said that, Williams exploded. He started screaming and cussing. "You lying SOB," he said, calling Kunkel every name in the book and a few that aren't there. Kunkel was screaming back all the time while the phone was in his hand, with MacPhail on the other end. Evidently MacPhail hadn't known Williams was in the room, but he knew it then.

MacPhail asked to talk to Red and then told Red to get Williams out of there and to call him later. Nothing ever happened, except for that big argument, and it really was brought on by Kunkel not wanting people to think Chalk was questioning his strike calls.

On another night, in Chicago, I enjoyed watching Williams embarrass himself and get in trouble. He accidentally copied his lineup card from the previous night, including Nolan Ryan pitching. Ryan had started the night before, but he had to pitch to at least one batter because he was listed as the starting pitcher.

The most famous incident in recent baseball history involving pine tar came in 1983, when George Brett was called out for having too much pine tar on his bat after hitting a home run in the ninth inning against the Yankees.

I was in Seattle when the original play happened, and of course it made all of the highlight shows because of the now-famous image of Brett charging out of the dugout when home-plate umpire Tim McClelland ejected him.

I think Brett might have killed McClelland if he had not been restrained by teammates, coaches, and crew chief Joe Brinkman. After the home run was overturned and Brett declared out, the Yankees went on to win the game. The Royals protested, and MacPhail upheld the protest. He ruled that the home run should be allowed to stand, claiming "games should be won and lost on the playing field, not through technicalities of the rules."

I agreed with MacPhail. Other umpires did not. I had the advantage of having had time to read the rule book, and I didn't feel there was a penalty established for having too much pine tar on the bat. The rule book said you couldn't have it, but it didn't say you should be ejected or called out. Common sense also tells me that having extra pine tar on a bat cannot make a batter hit a home run.

Brett always had a heavy amount of pine tar on his bat. He did not wear batting gloves, and he constantly wrapped his hand around the pine tar on the top of his bat to help him get a better grip.

MacPhail's ruling was that the home run should stand and the game resumed at that point, with Kansas City leading 5–4 with two outs in the ninth. He scheduled the completion of the game for August 18, an off day for both teams.

Dick Butler, the supervisor of officials, called me and said he wanted my crew to work the completion of the game. I didn't want to do it. We were going to start a series in Baltimore the next day with a doubleheader. Sharon and the girls were with me, and we had planned to spend the off day in Washington, including going to the White House and doing other tourist activities. But Butler insisted, so I had to do it. I knew it was going to be an ugly scene because George Steinbrenner was furious and Billy Martin, then the manager of the Yankees, was just as mad.

The completion of the game was scheduled for 4:30 P.M. The Royals' charter plane landed at Newark, and Brett didn't even leave the plane. He stayed there, playing cards with team officials who didn't make the journey into Yankee Stadium either.

When we got to the dressing room, one of the A.L. officials, Bob Fishel, came in to greet us. I didn't want to be there, and I was really ticked off and disgusted that I had to give up my off day for this charade. Bob was about to make the day more interesting.

"We have reason to believe the Yankees are going to protest the game," Fishel said. "They are going to claim that Brett missed first base when he was running around the bases two months ago."

I just stared at Fishel, letting him continue. "They know you weren't here, that it was other umpires. I'm going to give you an affidavit to keep in your pocket in case this happens. The affidavit is a court document stating that the four umpires who were at the game saw Brett touch not only first, but second, third, and home as well.

"If Martin comes out and says he is going to protest the game, you show him the affidavit."

I folded it and put it in my pocket, saying, "This isn't going to happen, is it?"

We got set to start the game, and I'll be darned if the Yankees' pitcher, George Frazier, didn't step off the mound and throw to first. I was working second base, and a young umpire, Tim Welke, was at first. Welke gave the safe sign, and here came Martin, charging out of the dugout.

He was headed straight for Welke, and I knew all too well he was going to jump all over the younger umpire. I came toward Martin and intercepted him.

"Davey, Davey, I know you were in Seattle, but I'm telling you Brett missed first base," Martin said.

I smiled and said, "Billy, let me tell you something. I was in Seattle, you are right, but I happen to have an affidavit—" He interrupted me: "An affi-f*****-what?"

I pulled the paper out of my pocket, slowly unfolded it, and showed it to Billy. That became a famous photograph and was the only time an affidavit had to be used in a major league game. I explained to Billy that the four umpires who were at the game had stated that Brett not only had touched first, but had also touched second, third, and home legally.

Billy stood there for a minute, not believing what had just happened and that he had lost his argument so quickly.

The last four outs of the game took 12 minutes and 16 pitches. I didn't even have to take a shower. But we missed out on going to the White House.

I know why Billy was so upset. He thought he had won his little battle with Brett and had outsmarted him, and instead he had lost. Billy was not a good loser.

The relationships between umpires and managers always provide interesting analysis. People on both sides hold grudges against each other, like Luciano and Weaver. Some managers are miserable, like Williams; some don't always use good judgment, like Maury Wills. Some are more volatile than others, and some are more likely to express their disagreement with a call. No umpire ever likes to eject a player or manager from a game, but a lot of times he really has no other choice—especially when someone just questioned whether his mother and father were married when he was born; thought his first name was "mother"; or decided to try being a sumo wrestler and slam into him.

6

Tantrums

The manager who seems to have the most violent temper tantrums these days is Lou Piniella, now with the Tampa Bay Devil Rays. This has never come as a surprise to me, because I remember him first as a player, and he had quite a temper then too. Umpires did not look forward to working behind the plate when Piniella was playing. He had a reputation for thinking that a pitch was a strike only when he swung. When he took the pitch, he thought it should be a ball, and he usually had no problem telling exactly that to the home-plate umpire.

About my third year in the league, I worked a game at first base and realized that I would have the plate the next day for Piniella. I lay awake late that night, trying to think of a way to handle him. Finally, I came up with a plan I thought would work.

There were no problems during his first couple of at-bats, but the next time up he took a pitch that I called a ball. He swiveled around in my direction and very bluntly said, "Where the f*** was that pitch at?"

I called time, took off my mask, and stared back at him.

"Lou, Lou, Lou, I can't believe you. Don't you know you never, never, ever, ever end a sentence with a preposition?" I said.

I could tell Lou was totally confused. "What?" he finally said. "What are you talking about?"

"You never ever end a sentence with a preposition," I repeated. "You said, 'Where was the pitch at?' *At* is a preposition, and you never end a sentence with a preposition."

Piniella didn't know what to say. I was feeling pretty proud of myself as he stepped back into the batter's box. Suddenly he raised his hand and yelled "time."

I raised my hand and granted his request. He stepped out of the box and said, "I would like to rephrase that question."

Without waiting for me to acknowledge him, Lou said, "Where was that f****** pitch at, you asshole?" I ejected him.

Piniella, of course, was no stranger to ejections, as either a player or a manager. I have been witness to some volatile displays over the years from Billy Martin, Earl Weaver, Dick Williams, and others, but Piniella gets as mad as anybody when he really gets going. Martin would pick up the dirt and throw it. Weaver had to be carried off the field one time by Ken Kaiser and Nick Bremigan. Williams was the most sarcastic manager I ever knew. Larry Barnett almost threw his arm out of place one time when he was kicking Williams out of a game. I've always said one of the highlights of my career was when Williams left the American League to manage in the N.L. in Montreal—I wasn't sad to see him leave the country.

One thing all of those managers had in common was their ability to intimidate young umpires. They thought the louder they were, the more violent they were, the more cuss words they used, the more they would be able to influence an umpire. They thought they might not win that argument, but the next time, a questionable call might go their way. Most of the good umpires that I know, however, think exactly the opposite. A manager or a player who builds that kind of reputation is going to have a lot of problems getting along with umpires.

One young umpire whom managers thought they could intimidate was Dale Scott, my partner for many years. Those managers were wrong. Dale is very intelligent, and he can go toe-to-toe with the best of them. He had better answers in an argument than any manager could ever come up with. I had to step in between him and Sparky Anderson one time in a game in Toronto, and I thought I was in a bumper car the way they kept going back and forth.

Dale was also behind the plate in Seattle for one of Piniella's big tirades. That scene reminded me of a time early in my career in Chicago when I watched veteran umpire Chris Pelekondas. Leo Durocher was going crazy and kicking dirt all over the place. Chris never moved. He just stood there like nothing was happening. I couldn't believe his composure. When a manager or player is standing there kicking dirt at an umpire, the first reaction, after the ejection, is to kick back. I have done it, and so have most of the umpires I know.

As I watched Pelekondas that day, however, I decided that that might be a better way to handle such a situation. And that's what I thought of the day Piniella started going crazy with Dale. As the crew chief, I walked in toward the plate. Dale was giving it right back to Piniella, until I got there and motioned for him not to say anything. "Let's let him make a fool of himself," I said, which wasn't all that hard for Lou when he was mad.

So Dale and I just stood there, with our hands on our chins, as Piniella proceeded to kick dirt all over the plate. When he got tired, he got down on his knees and scooped dirt over the plate with his hands. When he had the plate sufficiently covered, he took off his cap and threw it. He finally started walking off the field, kicking his cap toward the dugout. It was quite a show. Even though Lou can go crazy, I personally liked him and enjoyed working for him when he was a manager. When he was a player, that was a different story.

Williams was managing Oakland when I had the first ejection of my career—Reggie Jackson. The A's were playing Boston in the *Game of the Week* in late May of my first season, 1971. I was working second base and was most excited because it was the first game I had worked that was going to be on national television. I knew Sharon and all of my family would be able to watch the game in St. Louis.

It was a terrible game, with a lot of runs and errors. It was a typically long American League game. Reggie wasn't having a very good day either. He was at first base when a ball was hit to right field. Reggie had rounded second a bit too far and had to scramble to get back to second as the Red Sox got the ball back into the infield. He took a little too long, and he was tagged out. He started screaming, and I ejected him.

After the game, I called home and asked Sharon what she thought of the game. "What did you think about the ejection?" I said. "What ejection?" she said.

It turned out she had left the television to change our seven-month-old daughter Jill's diaper at that particular moment and missed it. So much for my national television debut.

Reggie turned out to be a good friend, and I think we developed a great deal of respect for each other. He was the greatest clutch player I saw during my career. He definitely had a flair for the dramatic moment, and he loved being in the spotlight. I happened to be working in Boston the day he played the final game of his career at Fenway Park. He came up as a pinch-hitter and got a nice ovation from the crowd. He was standing, waving, and I waited for him to enjoy the moment before telling him to get in the box to hit. It was a Sunday, a getaway day.

After the game I was back in our dressing room, hurrying to catch a plane, when there was a knock on the door. A kid was there and he said, "Dave Phillips?" I said yes and he handed me a bat. "Reggie wants you to have this." It was the bat he had used that day, and he had autographed it to me. I really appreciated the gesture. That was typical of him— always dramatic.

When I ejected Reggie in my first year, Williams came out to argue, but he couldn't really say much because it was such an obvious play. Another time, though, I was working first base and he came out to argue a checked-swing call. This was before the rule change making it mandatory for an umpire to check on half swings. He didn't ask me a question, he just said, "You know he swung."

He proceeded to walk to second, where Barnett was working, and as he got close to Larry he said, "I'm not even going to ask this piece of shit." Larry ejected Williams and almost threw his arm out. I was trying not to laugh out loud.

Williams had to walk past third, where Chylak was working, on his way to the clubhouse. Most good crew chiefs would have gotten in the middle of the argument as soon as Williams walked on the field, but Nestor of course just stood there. Instead, when Williams got near Chylak, Williams told him, "It's a shame you have to work with this shit."

Of course, we all thought it was a shame we had to work with Chylak. We didn't really mind being referred to as his three sons, if it meant we could have run away from home. Nestor was responsible, however, for one of the funniest moments of that season.

We were in Baltimore, and Nestor's wife and kids were there because he was going home after our series ended. We all piled into his car to ride from the hotel to the stadium, and he stopped for gas. As the pump clicked off, some gas spilled onto the pavement.

Nestor started screaming and going nuts, and the station attendant came out. "I'm not paying for that gas," Nestor was screaming, pointing to the gas that had spilled. "That's at least $2 worth of gas on the ground."

The attendant looked at how much gas had spilled, and said, "That's maybe five cents' worth of gas, sir."

Nestor was adamant that it was at least $2 worth and wanted to be reimbursed. The attendant went over to the pump, turned the gauge back to zero, and proceeded to release the nozzle and let gas start pouring onto the pavement.

Nestor, of course, was screaming again. "What are you doing? Are you crazy?" he yelled. We were all laughing our heads off. The guy stopped the pump after spraying five cents' worth of gas on the pavement. That was his way of responding to Chylak's argument. Nestor had had a cigarette in his mouth the whole time—if he had dropped it, what a picture that would have made of a gas station explosion! Earl would have loved it.

One of the funniest incidents I ever saw on the field, which also produced a big argument, came a few years later in Seattle during a game between Kansas City and the Mariners.

Amos Otis was batting, and he hit the ball off the end of his bat, a slow roller down the third-base line. Lenny Randle was playing third for the Mariners, and he came in, but then decided to let the ball roll. As it was rolling, Lenny got down on his knees and crawled next to the ball. I was watching this from my position near second base.

Larry McCoy was working the plate, and he finally yelled and signaled that it was a foul ball. Jim Frey, the Royals' manager, came running out from the dugout. The third-base coach was screaming, and as I got closer to the argument, I heard him yell, "He blew the ball foul."

McCoy had a real befuddled look on his face, like maybe he agreed with the coach. "Hold on a minute," I said to everybody and took McCoy off to the side, away from the coaches and players. "What happened, Mac?" I said.

"It was the damnedest thing I've ever seen," McCoy said. "He was crawling along with the ball, and he started blowing on the ball. He kept blowing." I said he couldn't do that. "Did he blow the ball foul?" I asked. McCoy said, "Yeah, I think he did."

I turned back around and pointed that Otis was going to be awarded first base. That of course meant the Kansas City side was happy, but now I had another argument, with Seattle manager Rene Lachemann.

To my knowledge there is no rule that says you can't blow on the ball, but common sense tells you that you can't change the course of a ball. That's what he did.

After I explained my reasoning to Lachemann, he went over to Randle. He said, "Did you blow on the ball?" I am sure he was hoping the answer would be no. "Skipper, I never blew on the ball," Randle said. "All I did was yell *'Go foul! Go foul!'* " As soon as he said that, everybody broke up laughing, and the argument was over.

Another time we were in Seattle I had to change a home-run call. At that time Lachemann was being criticized for never arguing with umpires. He had grown up in baseball, having worked as a batboy for the Dodgers, and I thought he was a good guy and fair. He once told me he always had respect for umpires after my old friend, Stan Landes, threw his plate shoes at Rene, who was a batboy at the time, because he had not shined Stan's shoes.

When we changed the call, Lachemann came out to argue. He was talking more than he was arguing, but he was being real demonstrative with his hands and arms. He said, "I'm telling you guys I have to be ejected. You have to eject me. Everybody is on me about not arguing and being ejected enough."

I said, "We can handle that," and Steve Palermo ejected him. He put on a little more of a show, and then went in the dugout and started tossing everything he could get onto the field—the Gatorade jug, bats, gloves, it didn't matter. It was a little more of a show than anyone expected.

The next day, Lachemann came over to our dressing room before the game, laughing. I said, "It was one thing for you to ask us to eject you, but it was another to throw all that crap on the field. Ejection is one thing, cleaning up the field is another."

Lachemann laughed and then explained, "I don't get ejected that much, and I've seen guys do that on television, so I thought I should do it too." He was acting too much like Piniella.

Those were the kinds of problems I expected when Billy Martin got mad. Earlier in my career, I was working a game in Detroit when Martin was there. Bill Freehan was catching. Martin was wearing a microphone and was being taped for a show to be broadcast during the All-Star Game, but I didn't know that at the time. There was a runner on first, and he was stealing second. The batter fouled off the pitch, and Freehan caught it.

Larry Napp was working first base, and I guess he didn't understand the signal for a foul tip. He signalled it a foul ball and was telling the runner to go back to first. Ted Williams and Nellie Fox were arguing the call. Napp asked if I had called it a foul ball. I said no, it was a foul tip; the runner should stay at second. Out came Martin to argue; in front of me, he yelled at Freehan, "*You dropped the ball, didn't you?*" Freehan said, "No, Skip, I caught it."

I didn't know about Martin being taped until the All-Star break, when the show was broadcast. On the tape, when Martin got back to the dugout, he walked up and down the bench yelling at everybody. "When I come out and ask you if something happened, you always agree with me."

Freehan was not a bad guy. I just always hoped Tom Haller was catching whenever I worked Detroit. He was umpire Bill Haller's brother, a great catcher and a great guy. Freehan was always questioning calls, but I know it wasn't his idea. He was only doing what Martin was telling him to do.

I had to eject Freehan one time when Ralph Houk was managing. I think the Tigers had lost 20 games in a row, and everybody was upset. In the first inning, there was a walk or two before we got an out, and Freehan said something sarcastic. I stepped out in front of the plate and made it clear that I had heard enough. One more sarcastic comment and he would be ejected. He said "f*** you" and *boom*, he was ejected.

The funniest part of the story was that before the game, Freehan had received a huge trophy for being named "Mr. Congeniality." There was a small picture on the front page of the sports section in the Detroit newspaper the next day. There was a note that said to turn to page two for the results of the game, and there was a large photo of me ejecting Freehan. The caption said Freehan was the first out of the game, *thrown out.*

Martin was always much tougher on his catchers than Houk, making them complain about calls and constantly wanting them to question the umpire. It happened a few years later when Martin was managing Oakland. Mike Heath was the catcher.

I was working first base, and Lou DiMuro was behind the plate. The whole night, Heath kept questioning pitches. Lou was such a polite man, he should have been a priest.

I don't think he ever enjoyed the job of umpiring. He was a nice man, and didn't relish the thought of arguing with players or managers. I was so upset that I would have ejected Heath from first base, but I didn't want to embarrass Lou.

The next day, Lou went home because he had an injury to his hip. I was still very upset when we got to home plate for the exchange of the lineup cards because of the unprofessional way Heath had treated Lou the night before. I always believed that what happened in a previous game was over, and the next night was a new night, but that night I was determined to teach Heath a lesson.

Clete Boyer was coaching for Oakland, and when he brought out the lineup card I said, "I'll tell you what, Clete. You tell Billy that he better have another catcher ready soon because I will run Heath if he says one f****** word to me." Clete thought I was kidding. "Clete, you and I are friends, but I am dead serious," I said.

Mike came running out when the A's took the field, and he was all smiling and happy. "Hey guys, what's going on?" he said. I was hot. "Let me tell you something, you f****** jerk." I just exploded at him. The national anthem was being played, he was standing next to me, and I called him everything except his first name. It was terrible. I am embarrassed that I did it, but I was so upset from the night before that it had to be done.

Mike was stunned. I knew why he had done it; Martin abused DiMuro, and he knew DiMuro wouldn't eject him. Mike was doing what he was told.

The A's were playing the Yankees, and Bobby Murcer was the first batter. Murcer really had a confused look on his face because he had no idea what was going on with all of the yelling and screaming. I was still yelling at Heath as the pitch was coming to the plate. Bobby had to step out because he said he couldn't possibly hit with me screaming like that.

We finally got through the inning, and Martin began screaming at Heath in the dugout. You could tell Heath was confused. He didn't know what was going on. Billy came out of the dugout and told me he was going to take Heath out of the game. I literally begged Martin, "Don't take him out of the game. Let me eject him."

Billy said, "I don't want you upset." But it was a little late for that.

Another manager that I had more than my share of arguments with, of course, was Earl Weaver. One time we were in Baltimore, and about 40 minutes before the game, Bill Kunkel announced that he didn't feel well and could not work the game. He got up and walked out of the dressing room. We thought he was kidding. It was about time to start the game, and we walked out of the dressing room and asked the guard if he had seen Kunkel.

"You just missed him," the guard said. "He got in a cab and left."

Kunkel had been set to umpire the plate, and suddenly I had to replace him. I was really aggravated. In the first inning, Lee May came to bat for Baltimore, and he turned around to question a call. I looked at him and he said, "Man, what you got the red ass about?"

I started to answer him, but by that time Weaver had come out. He was just about the last person I wanted to see. "Earl, let me tell you something," I said. "I am in no f****** mood for you, so you had better go and leave me alone." He started kicking dirt on me, and I kicked it back on him. He got to go home.

One of the most interesting years I ever had as an umpire was 1976, when I was working with DiMuro, Kunkel, and Rich Garcia. For some reason we worked a lot of Cleveland games early in the year and we had a lot of problems with them, including their manager, Frank Robinson. They gave our crew the nickname DiMuro's Destroyers.

In one game, I ejected Buddy Bell when he complained about a called third strike. When Robinson came out to argue, he had pretty much decided that our crew had it out for the Indians, which wasn't the case at all. I told Frank why Bell had been ejected, and he didn't say anything, but he started walking toward the mound. I followed him and said, "Frank, where are you going?" He said, "I don't want to talk to you."

He walked past the mound and went all the way past second base where DiMuro was standing. Frank stood there and pleaded with DiMuro, "You are the crew chief. You have got to stop this." DiMuro just stood there. I caught up with them in short center field and stepped in between Frank and DiMuro. I said, "Frank," and he didn't look at me. I kept talking. "*You have just been ejected.*" He was still talking to DiMuro and ignoring me. "Frank, I don't know if you heard me, but you've just been ejected."

It was the first time as a plate umpire I ejected someone in short center field. It was kind of embarrassing, but I had to do it. By May 30, our crew had 13 ejections of the Indians and none of them were for fights or arguments. I wasn't surprised that we didn't work another Cleveland game that year.

I did share a funny moment with Robinson later, however. I was working a game at second base, and a ball was hit down the left-field line. Duane Kuiper was playing second for the Indians, and I could tell there was going to be a play made on the runner and it was going to be close. Kuiper caught the throw and dove toward the runner, creating a big pile of dust. I was right on top of the play, and I kept yelling to Kuiper, "Let me see the ball, let me see the ball" before I made the call.

Usually in that situation an umpire thinks the fielder has dropped the ball, and if so, the runner is safe. I guess that was kind of what I expected, and then Kuiper held up his glove, with the ball still in it. Then I signalled, "*Safe.*" Kuiper had a bewildered look on his face, and Robinson came trotting out. Both wanted to know why I needed to see the ball if I was going to call the runner safe anyway. I had no idea. I told Frank, "I guess I wanted to see the ball, but I thought he was safe." He really couldn't argue with that logic.

One manager whom I don't think I ever ejected was Gene Mauch, but we did have some good arguments over the years.

Gene was very respectful of umpires, and he also viewed himself as an expert on the rules—until a game one day in Anaheim. The Twins were playing the Angels, and Rod Carew was on first. I was working at second. The ball was hit to left-center, and it looked for sure like it was going to be a double or triple. Carew was running hard, and I know he was hoping he could score on the play. The center fielder, however, came out of nowhere and made a miraculous catch.

Mauch was coaching third as he often did, and he was screaming for Carew to stop and get back to first. Carew was almost to third. He looked and saw what was happening and headed back to first—unfortunately, right across the pitcher's mound. It looked like it was going to be a close play at first, even though I knew Carew would be out because he had failed to retouch second on his way back to first.

Unbelievably, the throw to first was wild and went into the dugout. By rule, Carew was awarded third base, which was the correct ruling. Dick Williams was managing the Angels, and he came storming out of the dugout. Williams obviously knew Carew had missed second base on his return to first, so he instructed the pitcher to appeal the play to second and he did, and I called Carew out.

Mauch did everything but cartwheels coming toward me, and we had a big argument. He protested the game. Afterward, all of the writers, after looking up the rules, went up to him and told him he was wrong, that I had called the play correctly. I guess he was embarrassed, and the next night I went directly to the Twins' dugout before the game so he could see me. He came over and said, "I've never seen that play before" and walked away. He could not admit that he was wrong; only that he had never seen the play.

Our crew had a couple of other run-ins with Mauch over the years, even though I really liked Gene. He appreciated guys who could umpire, and he liked guys who hustled. One day in Milwaukee, I was working third base when

Robin Yount hit a ball to left field. I honestly could not tell if it went over the wall or not because it looked like it might have hit the rail on the very top of the wall. I called it a home run, but Yount didn't slow up and the left fielder hurried and got the ball and threw it back toward the infield. Yount was trying for an inside-the-park homer, and it was going to be a close play. Jerry Neudecker was working the plate, and thank God he called Yount safe or we would have had a gigantic argument.

Mauch came running out to question my call, and all I could tell him was that the ball looked to me like it was out of the park. He then argued it should not have been my call anyway. Steve Palermo was working second, and Mauch insisted that it should have been his call. There really shouldn't have been an argument at all because Yount was safe, anyway. It was still a home run.

While talking to Palermo, Mauch suddenly went nuts. He was screaming, and he normally didn't do that. When I got a chance, I went over to Steve and said, "What did you say to Mauch?"

Palermo said he told him, "You know what, Gene, arguing with you is like dueling with an unarmed man." I wanted to laugh so bad, but I couldn't find a place where I could hide. Mauch, being a macho guy and authoritative person, liked Steve, but he didn't like being called an unarmed man.

A similar thing happened one night with Bill Kunkel. Mauch had come from the National League, and there was a difference between the two leagues concerning where the second-base umpire stood on stolen-base attempts. The A.L. umpires stood outside the base line, and Mauch never thought we were in the proper position to make the call. He bitched about it so much he later got it changed so that we had to work on the infield.

On this night, there was a steal attempt and the call went against Mauch, and he came trotting out for a routine argument. All of a sudden it was like somebody had poured gasoline on Mauch, he was going so crazy. Mauch had to be restrained and then practically dragged off the field. When the argument was over, I asked Kunkel why Mauch got so mad.

Kunkel said, "I just told him I watched him manage in '64, and he screwed up then and he was wrong here too." I could see why Mauch was so upset—he really didn't want people reminding him of the Phillies' collapse in 1964, when they lost a seven-game lead in the final week of the season and saw the Cardinals win the pennant.

Another manager I had a great deal of respect for was Dick Howser, whom I got to know very well when he was coaching third for the Yankees. I was surprised he even wanted to be a manager, but it turned out he did a great job. He was the manager of the Royals when I went with them on a trip to Japan after the 1981 season, and he almost caused me to create an international incident.

Dick and I and our wives went to dinner on one of our first nights in Japan, and he commented that he had heard it was not unusual for managers in Japan to slap an umpire and have 20-minute arguments. I had heard some of the same things.

"Let me tell you something, Dick," I said. "No one is going to come out and slap me in the face."

A day or two later, the Royals were playing the Tokyo Giants, and I was behind the plate. I called one of the Giants out on strikes. He didn't say anything, but I could tell by the way he looked at me that he didn't like it. As the next hitter was walking to the plate, Howser yelled from the Kansas City dugout, "Here he comes, Davey."

I looked toward the Giants' dugout, and their manager was walking directly toward me. I jumped in front of him and screamed as loud as I could, "*Don't you come another step.*" It scared him, and he jumped back like he was stunned. He immediately turned around and went back to the dugout.

I put my mask on and got back behind John Wathan, the catcher for the Royals, and the next hitter stepped into the box. I immediately realized I didn't recognize the batter. Apparently the manager wasn't coming out to argue or slap me in the face; he was coming out to tell me he was sending up a pinch-hitter. I am certain he was back in the dugout talking about the crazy American umpire.

I thought the world of Howser because he was a great people person. I'll never forget one time when he was managing the Yankees. They had a backup catcher, Rick Cerone, who was giving umpires trouble, and I told him our crew wasn't going to put up with it. Howser tried to act as mediator, and he asked if he could set up a meeting with me, Cerone, and my crew.

I told Cerone, "If you want to get along with the umpires, we have a very simple set of rules. You treat us with respect and we will treat you with respect."

Cerone said, "Well, I used to see [Thurman] Munson yell." I said, "Number one, you didn't see Munson yell at me, and number two, you're not Thurman Munson." He didn't have a comeback for that one.

I have ejected a lot of managers and players for a lot of different reasons. I kicked Will Clark out of a game one time when he ignored my request to give me the ball after the third out of an inning and threw it into the stands instead. I also saw my partner and good friend Steve Palermo eject Lou Whitaker of the Tigers for smiling at him.

I was working at second; Steve was at third. We were chatting between innings, and all of a sudden Steve said, "Dave, if Lou Whitaker runs by me one more time and smiles, I am going to eject him." Evidently, Lou had baited Steve. Every time Lou came on and left the field he would run by Steve with a big smile on his face, and for some reason it was upsetting Steve.

Sure enough, the next inning, here came Lou with a big smile and Steve said, "That's it," and ran him. Lou continued running out to his position at second base. He didn't know he had been ejected. Sparky was down in the tunnel smoking his pipe, and he didn't see what happened. Palermo was screaming at Whitaker, "Don't you smile at me." Finally Sparky came running out wanting to know what happened.

"You better get your second baseman off the field because he has been ejected," I told Sparky. "What did he do?" Sparky asked. At that exact moment, Lou said, "I love you, Stevie." Steve was still yelling, "I don't want you to love me." Sparky eventually got Lou to leave, but by then the Tigers were really upset.

Jim Campbell, the general manager, was furious. He called everyone in the league office he could call. I had no more walked into my hotel room when the phone rang. It was Dick Butler, wanting to know what happened.

"Don't tell me you don't know what happened," Butler said. "Did Steve run him because he smiled at him?" I said I didn't know exactly what had happened and that he should call Steve. Butler was upset at my answer, but Steve was my partner and I wanted him, not me, to tell Butler what took place.

Sparky came out to argue another time when he thought I missed a call. The Tigers were playing Kansas City, and Willie Wilson made a snow-cone catch. You could see the ball right at the edge of his glove. As he reached into his glove to remove the ball, he dropped it. I was within 10 feet of him, and I called it a catch. Sparky came running out, and I was ready for him. "What the f*** do you want?" I yelled.

I started to dress him down, because that was the common practice of umpires in those days—to go on the offensive in arguments instead of being defensive. "You saw what happened. I know what happened, and you know what happened," I said. It really embarrassed Sparky, and I felt bad about that. Managers, especially when they are at home, don't want to be embarrassed. Sparky was a good people person and I always respected him, but his managerial style was a lot of show. I thought he handled his players well, except for Jack Morris.

Another manager who got mad at me one time was Pat Corrales, when he was working in Cleveland. There was a balk called by the home-plate umpire, and Pat came out to argue. I walked down from first base, and he started walking back up the line with me. I had accomplished my goal of getting him away from the younger umpire, and as we walked I said, "Pat, it's time to go." He said he wasn't leaving, so I ejected him.

He went to the dugout and took the show a little too far, like Lachemann had done, throwing things out of the dugout. It was a good thing I was watching him, because all of a sudden a bat came flying out of the dugout and was heading straight for my head. I ducked, and the bat landed in the infield.

I could tell as soon as he let the bat go he did not mean to throw it. When the game ended, I was back in our dressing room and the phone rang. It was Pat, apologizing for throwing the bat. I believe he was sincere and not calling just to get out of a fine or suspension. It was as close as I ever came to being hit by a flying bat. Other than that one moment, Pat was always really professional, and I appreciated that.

We were working in Cleveland one time on a brutally hot day. I had the plate, and about the fourth or fifth inning, I was standing behind the plate in between innings sweating. The Indians' mascot walked right in front of me and began squirting me in the face with a water pistol. I suppose it was funny to the few people in the stands, but I was furious. I started screaming and called the mascot every name I could think of. I was really hot, and not just from the weather.

After the game, we got dressed and were ready to leave the stadium when one of the police officers I knew asked if he could talk to me. I stopped, and I noticed this young girl was with him. She was a cute girl, maybe 16 or 17 years old. The officer said the girl wanted to talk to me, and I graciously said, "OK, what can I do for you?"

She said, "Mr. Phillips, I just wanted to say I am really sorry for squirting you with the water." She was the mascot. I didn't know who was inside that costume, and it was this young girl. I had called her every name in the book, and now I was apologizing to her after she came to apologize to me.

One player who never apologized and never had an umpire apologize to him was Alex Johnson. He might have been the most difficult person I ever dealt with in the game. He could hit, but what a jerk. I have often said that he was the only player who if I ever walked out of a stadium and saw him standing there, I would turn around and walk back in the stadium.

He had won the American League batting title in 1970, the year before I came up to the majors, beating out Carl Yastrzemski by one point. The next year, however, when we came into Anaheim in May, he was loafing, and manager Lefty Phillips had benched him. The Angels had a bat day promotion featuring Johnson bats, and Alex was sitting in a corner of the dugout with his leg up, sulking. It looked like he was asleep.

When he was in the mood, Johnson would run to his position in the outfield but make it look like he was going to run into an umpire. He would run right at him, then veer off to the side at the very last moment, trying to scare the umpire. He never did it to me, but I saw him do it. I know he had done it to Bill Haller, and then one night I watched him try to do it to Joe Brinkman.

Joe is definitely a man's man. He is as tough as nails and won't bend an inch. Johnson picked the wrong umpire. He ran at Joe, and Joe kicked him out of the game.

After the game, we were walking up the tunnel toward our dressing room, and who was standing there waiting for us, blocking our way, but a seminude Alex Johnson. He looked like a black Superman. He screamed at Joe, and I really thought he was going to start a fight or something, but he let us pass and nothing happened.

I brought Johnson up at an umpires union meeting that winter. I said, "I think somebody is going to get hurt by this guy." John Rice, who had been in the league a long time, stood up and agreed with me. He said he had been working home plate one time in Detroit when Johnson was batting, and when Freehan went out to talk to the pitcher, it was just Johnson and Rice standing there. All of a sudden, Rice said he heard Johnson say, "Boy, something sure smells like shit around here." That's the kind of stuff he did.

A different night, Larry McCoy had to go into the Tigers' training room to get a Band-Aid or aspirin or something before a game, and Johnson was there. When McCoy came back out of the room, he was fuming. We asked what had happened, and McCoy said when he walked into the room, Johnson said, "Well, look at the shit they let work the f****** plate tonight."

I only had a couple of games in my career when I threatened to call the police onto the field. Once in the minors, I ejected coach Herm Starrette from a game and he said he wouldn't leave. I was friends with the police officers in Richmond, Virginia, who were there, and I motioned for them to come onto the field. As they started to climb over the fence, Starrette took off running.

The other time was when Hal McRae was managing Kansas City. The Royals were playing Seattle on national television, and there was a ball hit down the left-field line that was clearly foul, but Dale Scott, who was working third, lost it in the lights and signaled it fair. I was working the plate, and Dale came down and asked me what I had seen, and I called it a foul ball. McRae came out, and one of his problems as a manager was that he really didn't know how to argue.

I told him, "Mac, it's a foul ball now and it's going to be a foul ball when we get done arguing, so it's time for you to go." He agreed, but he continued to argue because he didn't want me to reverse Dale's call. He said he wasn't leaving until I changed it back, and I motioned to the police officers standing behind the screen. One of the Royals coaches, Jamie Quirk, sized up the situation and helped McRae off the field before the cops could get there.

But one of the funniest stories I ever heard about how to break up an argument happened in Toronto. Marty Springstead was the crew chief, and Durwood Merrill was in the argument with Bobby Cox at the plate. As Marty came trotting in to intervene, he got about three feet away from the group and stubbed his toe on the AstroTurf. He crashed right into the middle of the group. Suddenly the argument was over.

Sometimes arguments are not solved by an umpire, and that's when the two teams take matters into their own hands and a fight breaks out on the field. It's something you never want to happen, but it does.

7

Brawls and Beanballs

Sometimes an umpire can see a fight coming. Other times, there is no warning.

I have been involved in several serious fights during my career, and I came away from each one with the feeling that it was totally unnecessary. I had one goal every time a fight broke out when I was on the field—to not get knocked out and then have a player say he was sorry.

Putting an end to brawls on the field is something the baseball leadership could do very easily, if it tried, but so far they have not come up with a plan to do so.

Since Frank Robinson became the disciplinarian for baseball, a job now held by Bob Watson, they have done a much better job of issuing fines and suspensions for those involved in fights, but that to me is not a preventive plan. I agree that you have to discipline people who get involved with the fights, but that is not the way to prevent them.

One of the worst fights I was ever involved in came on April 27, 1975, in the second game of a doubleheader in Anaheim between the Angels and the Oakland A's. Dick Williams was managing the Angels, and Whitey Herzog was his third-base coach. The Angels were leading 5–1 going into the sixth inning, and they scored four more runs that inning to build the lead to 9–1. In those days, if there was a lopsided score, teams did not try to continue stealing bases, which would humiliate the other team.

The Angels had a pretty young team with a lot of players they were trying to develop, and one of their strategies was to run as much as possible. During that sixth inning, I heard Williams yell from the bench out to Herzog, "Run their f****** tits off, Whitey."

On the next pitch, the Oakland pitcher, Jim Todd, drilled Bruce Bochte of the Angels right in the head, and the fight was on. The A's hated Williams because he had been their manager, and they welcomed the chance to go after him. When Dick led the charge out of the Angels' dugout onto the field, I don't think his young players knew to follow him, or else they didn't want to. It was really a funny sight, because I know Williams thought they would follow him, and when they didn't, he looked like he was almost running in place. Angel Mangual led the charge against Williams, and it wasn't pretty. Sal Bando, Gene Tenace, Joe Rudi, Catfish Hunter, Reggie Jackson, Ray Fosse, and Billy North were among the players who participated. They kicked and pummeled Dick. I can honestly say I wasn't upset.

A few years later, I was working a game in Texas when another serious fight broke out, this one between the Rangers and the Kansas City Royals. George Brett, the Royals' All-Star third baseman, suffered a separated shoulder and had to miss six weeks in the middle of the season.

Texas had one of the greatest fighting teams in history. They had veteran players such as Willie Horton, John Ellis, Jim Fregosi, Pat Corrales, and others, and they were not going to take any lip or abuse from anybody. That fight started when Bump Wills of Texas got caught in a rundown between third and home. Darrell Porter was catching for Kansas City, and when he finally went to tag Wills, he jammed the ball into his back very hard. It was obvious he had tried to hurt Wills, just like when a batter is intentionally hit by a pitch. Looking back on it now with the knowledge that Porter had a lot of problems with drugs, I wonder if he was not on something that day. Wills took exception to it, as any player would have, and pushed Porter back. When Porter then went after Wills, both benches emptied and we had a mess.

Kansas City had Porter, Brett, Frank White, and John Mayberry, but they were no match for Texas. We couldn't stop the brawl. We had individual fights all over the field. When order finally was restored, Brett was holding his arm, and it turned out he was hurt badly.

I have often been surprised that more players aren't hurt in fights. After I helped break up another fight with the Angels a few years later, who was pulled off the bottom of the pile but two of the team's best young pitchers, Mark Langston and Chuck Finley, neither of whom had been pitching that game. What would Gene Autry, the owner of the Angels, have said if either of them had gotten seriously hurt in that fight and had not been able to pitch for a while?

The other serious fight I recall came years later, in 1993, also in the second game of a doubleheader—that may be another reason not to play doubleheaders—in Milwaukee, and again Oakland was involved.

It was the ninth inning of the second game, and my legs and back were killing me. Dennis Eckersley, who was almost automatic as Oakland's closer, came into the game. But Dennis got roughed up on this night, and Milwaukee came back and tied the game. Just what we needed—extra innings in the second game of a doubleheader.

Dale Scott was working the plate, and Eck thought he had missed a couple of pitches that he wanted called strikes. Dale ignored him, but as Eckersley was coming out of the game, he was still yelling, and Dale ejected him. Tony LaRussa was managing, and he came running out. I limped toward the plate as best I could because I was so tired that I could hardly walk.

Eckersley was getting his money's worth, yelling at Dale and calling him every name he could think of. I know I heard the words *no good, lousy,* and *gutless,* with a few additional adjectives thrown in. I was trying to hold Eck back to keep him away from Dale.

Eck made a noise with his mouth, and I really thought he was getting ready to spit in Dale's face. I felt the wind go across my face, and I was sure when I turned around I was going to see Dale's face wet from spit. All Eck had done, however, was make the noise that he was getting ready to spit. He never actually did it. I guess he wanted Dale to think he was going to spit so he would jump back. Dale thought the same thing.

For some reason, Phil Garner, the manager of the Brewers, was out of the dugout and standing there. I guess he was trying to argue with us to get Eck off the field so that we could get the game going. The argument had taken a little longer than we would have liked, but there was really no call for Garner to be out on the field saying that. Believe me, we wanted to get the game over as soon as possible.

While Garner was standing there, one of the Oakland players, Troy Neel, came charging out of the dugout and hit Garner like he was a linebacker making a tackle. It turned out Neel had been a linebacker in college at Texas A&M. At that moment both benches and bullpens emptied, and we had a donnybrook going. Why Neel came out to hit Garner like that I had no idea, and I'm convinced Garner didn't either. I am also sure Garner wished Neel had not hit him like that.

So many individual fights were going on that I know we didn't know who all was involved. I did see B. J. Surhoff of the Brewers get smoked when he was punched right in the face by Edwin Nunez, a pitcher on the A's. Blood was flying everywhere. Once order was restored, we put together the people we knew were involved, and I went over to Tony and listed all of the players on both teams who were going to be ejected. He said, "Wait a minute, what about this guy," and gave me the name of another Milwaukee player. I said, "He's gone too." I knew LaRussa and Garner would know more about who was involved than the umpires.

I went over to Garner and said the same thing, and he asked about another Oakland player and I ejected him too. Then I went back to both managers and said, "Anybody else?" That's exactly how I handled it. It didn't matter to me who got ejected or how many players we ejected; I just wanted to make sure neither side thought they had won the fight. A total of eight players were ejected.

We were all exhausted. Dale was just beside himself because, as the first umpire involved, it was his job to write up the report about what had happened to turn in to the league office. I told him he could come to my room and I would help him write the lengthy report. We were up until almost 6:00 A.M. getting the report completed. So much for two-hour games.

Fighting in baseball is a joke. There were several bench-clearing brawls in the 2003 season, and even though Bob Watson issued a lot of fines and suspensions, there was no talk about that putting an end to the fights. Basketball stopped it, football stopped it, and baseball could too. The problem is baseball doesn't want to address the problem, but instead wants to put the onus on the umpires to keep fights from happening.

The worst basketball fight I was ever involved with was a game between archrivals Kansas and Missouri. There must have been an earlier problem that year that caused it, because we had just tipped the game off and nothing had yet happened in the game. The game was in Lawrence, Kansas, and the players actually went under the stands punching each other. If the crowd had gotten involved we would have had a major problem.

Another major fight in college basketball occurred in a game between Minnesota and Ohio State, and it involved future major leaguer and Hall of Famer Dave Winfield. It was an ugly scene and went a long way toward bringing about the reforms in that sport's rules against fighting.

What administrators in college basketball knew is that the way you prevent something is by putting a rule in place that if anybody comes off the bench to join in a fight, that person will be suspended, and not just for a game or two. An umpiring crew can handle it when a pitcher and batter get into it, or something of that nature, because it usually is just a one-on-one situation. It's when you get 25 people on both sides involved that you have major problems.

Most fights start when a pitcher hits a batter or comes close to hitting a batter, and the batter thinks it is intentional. Baseball administrators think they have devised a way to stop those kinds of fights by instructing umpires when to issue warnings against a pitcher. Once a pitcher has been warned, the next time a pitch comes close to a batter and the umpire thinks it's intentional, the pitcher is ejected. That's the system Sandy Alderson has implemented, and everybody involved in the game—the umpires, the managers, and the players—know it is a joke.

It's unfortunate that people who never played or umpired the game are involved in making decisions about how the game should be played. That is a major mistake, in my opinion.

A couple of years ago Pedro Martinez was issued a warning in the second inning when he hit a batter in the back with a slow curveball. If Pedro wanted to hit somebody, he would hit him, and he wouldn't throw a curveball. He was one of the better pitchers I worked with over the years. He had tremendous control, threw strikes, and worked fast. I don't consider him a vicious guy. They called Bob Gibson a competitor, and he would knock a hitter down. They didn't call him vicious. Pedro is a throwback to pitchers like Gibson and Don Drysdale. He has the same mentality—he isn't afraid to throw inside.

Umpires are very talented and knowledgeable, and they know for the most part when a pitcher is intentionally trying to hit a batter. There doesn't have to be a rule to force them to put a warning in place. Umpires sometimes look foolish putting that warning in, and they are only doing it because they are forced to.

Baseball does have what is called a "heads-up" program now, and I think that is a good idea. Steve Palermo runs it, and basically he just makes certain any crew of umpires assigned to a series is made aware of any problems that a team has been having, or if there were any incidents the last time those two particular clubs played. That way umpires can be on the lookout for problems and try to get them stopped at the first sign of trouble.

We had an incident during the 1983 A.L. playoff series between the Orioles and the Chicago White Sox. Nick Bremigan was working the plate, and I was at second base. Somebody whizzed a pitch past Eddie Murray, and I could tell there was going to be retaliation. As the crew chief, I took over and told Bremigan we were issuing the warnings right then. Bremigan didn't want to do that, because he was worried that if there was a close pitch after we issued the warnings, he would have to eject a pitcher even if the pitch had not been intentional.

I said, "It doesn't matter if a batter is hit, as long as *we* don't believe it was intentional." I tried to convince him that just because you issue a warning doesn't mean it has to be an automatic ejection. It comes down to the judgment of the umpire. If in the umpire's judgment the pitch was intentional, it also shouldn't matter if it is a playoff game or the World Series—the pitcher should be ejected.

One pitcher who was a nightmare for umpires to work early in his career was Randy Johnson, because his pitching was so wild. There are a lot of guys like him, but he really had a hard time learning to throw strikes. Sandy Koufax was like that. Randy worked at it, and he became one of the best pitchers in the game. Not only did he learn to find home plate, but he was also able to throw strikes consistently. He was big enough and tough enough and scary enough that he really intimidated hitters. He is so big that when he steps toward home plate it looks like he is right on top of you. Once he learned to throw the ball in the strike zone he was unhittable.

I was working second base one night when he was pitching in Seattle in 1990 against Detroit, and when we got to the ninth inning I noticed everybody in the crowd was standing and cheering. It was as if something had happened in another game. I turned around to look at the scoreboard to see what I had missed, but there was nothing up there. I knew the crowd was yelling about something; I just didn't know what it was.

Finally I looked at the scoreboard long enough to figure it out. Johnson was pitching a no-hitter. He was so erratic and there had been so many Detroit runners on base I had no idea he was still pitching a no-hitter. He got it, too, after allowing six walks and having another runner reach on an error. It was the first no-hitter in the Mariners' history and the only no-hitter, so far, in Johnson's career. It was quite impressive to those of us who remember that early in his career, you had to be ready to duck at any moment when he was on the mound.

Although fights and beanballs can cause a lot of trouble, they aren't the only problems that I wish baseball's leadership would address. The issue with steroids and drugs is another.

8

Steroids and Other Drugs

It's impossible to know how many players have had their careers ruined because of drugs, but I can certainly understand how it happens. There is no doubt there were players who could have made it to the Hall of Fame but didn't, and drugs were the reason.

I was kind of naïve about drugs when I came to the major leagues. I was scared of needles when I had to take a shot as a youngster. A lot of the older umpires I worked with took what was called a greenie when they needed a little boost, and nobody thought anything about it. Trainers passed them around the dressing room like candy. I really wasn't a purist, but I just never felt I needed that extra boost. Hell, I was in my twenties and had all the energy I needed in those days.

One of the first times I ever smelled marijuana I had no idea what it was, just that it was a strange, pungent odor. I was in Yankee Stadium, working first base. In Yankee

Stadium there is a lot of room behind the plate, but there is very little foul ground along the base lines. Chris Chambliss was playing first for the Yankees, and I looked over at him and said, "What is that smell?" He glanced toward the stands, then back to me, with kind of an "are you serious?" look. "What is it?" I repeated. Chris nodded toward the seats and said, "They're smoking marijuana."

I looked into the stands, and sure enough I saw several people passing a joint around. They were very open about it, not trying to hide it at all. I couldn't believe it.

The fans smoking marijuana in the stands was just one reason I was never thrilled to be assigned to work games at Yankee Stadium. It was a very difficult stadium to work in. There was always a problem there, even though the stadium's history is truly very special. Games in the Midwest and West just always seemed to go much more smoothly. The thing I liked the most about games in New York was hearing Frank Sinatra singing "New York, New York" because that meant the game was over and I was walking off the field.

The drug problem in major league baseball really began in the late seventies and got really bad in the eighties. As is the case with a lot of issues, baseball was slow in recognizing and dealing with the problem, and unfortunately a lot of players got into very serious problems and didn't get the help they needed until their careers were ruined.

Part of the problem, I think, was that the drugs were so readily available. We all learned, too late, that many of the deals were made right in the stadium, with the pushers even being allowed in the locker room because they were working as vendors, caterers, delivery people, or in other similar jobs.

A lot of the problems in trying to curb the drug use in the major leagues can be placed on the players association. They always have an excuse. There was a host of issues about why they didn't want players to be tested for drugs, citing their civil liberties and privacy issues. What the union failed to realize, and still doesn't realize, is that baseball and the union leaders are hurting the very people they should be trying to help, the players, who are their clients.

Just as we started to hear about all of the cocaine problems that were coming into baseball, Bobby Brown, the president of the A.L., called a meeting of all the umpires. He is a cardiologist, so we knew he had knowledge and credibility when he spoke about drugs and their effects. What he said always stuck with me. He told us that if you tried cocaine once, you might be OK. If you ever took it a second time, however, you would be hooked. You could not get off it. You would always be out looking for that high because it made you feel so good, and there was no other way you could regain that feeling. He said you never would be able to attain the same high without cocaine.

The umpires volunteered to take drug tests—not to show the players up but to let the world know that although everyone thinks we're fat and have bad eyesight, by God we aren't on drugs.

One of the teams affected the most by drug problems in the early eighties was the Kansas City Royals. I had heard rumors that certain players were on drugs, but I certainly didn't have any hard evidence. I was working second base in one particular game, and Willie Wilson was playing left field. Nothing was happening at that point in the game. The pitcher looked in for his sign, and all of a sudden Wilson just started cursing and screaming. I couldn't imagine what was going on out there. I turned around and looked at him, and he was in a rage. He was livid at himself. At that moment, I knew he was on drugs.

I went with the Royals on a trip to Japan after the season, and it was a wonderful trip. One night I was headed to my hotel room, and I bumped into George Brett, who was in the next room. We both smelled marijuana coming from a room down the hall. Brett pounded on the door, trying to get the attention of the guys in the room.

What George and I both knew, but the others either didn't know or didn't care about, was that you don't want to get caught with drugs, even marijuana, when you are in a foreign country like Japan. The police over there couldn't care less that you are a major league player. They don't fool around with you. If you get caught over there, you are going to stay over there for a while.

Darrell Porter was another guy who I didn't know was having problems with drugs, until he checked himself in for rehab. I had first met him when he was a kid in Milwaukee's minor league system. When I was coming to the major leagues, I went to Arizona to learn how to use the outside protector and Darrell was one of the players in the league. He was always a tough kid and was a talented athlete who played with intensity and had a lot of potential.

There were a couple of times in his career when I know he acted the way he did because of drugs, for example, during the big fight in Texas between the Royals and the Rangers, and another time when he bumped Durwood

Merrill during an argument. Even years after his playing career ended, Porter still was being victimized by drugs. He died way too young in 2002.

Some of the players who had drug problems were well publicized. Steve Howe got chance after chance, and the reason was obvious—he was a left-handed reliever who could throw 95 mph. It was amazing to me that baseball allowed that to happen. Every team that got him thought they were going to be the one who could clean up Steve Howe. He wanted to do it too. He was truly a good guy, but the demons were just too great for him.

Both Doc Gooden and Darryl Strawberry had tremendous talent, but they never reached their full potential because of drugs, and that's sad and shameful.

Keith Hernandez was another player who I thought could have been a Hall of Famer had he not gotten himself hooked on drugs. It really was a shame because he was one of those players who could do it all—hit, hit for power, and field terrifically.

Of course, a lot of lesser players got messed up with drugs too. Alan Wiggins was one of the most arrogant players I ever knew, along with Alex Johnson. I ejected Wiggins one time when he was at first base because he was arguing that the pitcher was balking when he threw to first. He wouldn't let up. "I'll let you know if he balks," I said, and he indicated I was a mother, which was a physical impossibility.

Another time, I came into the umpires' dressing room in Oakland, about an hour and a half before the game, and I heard a noise in the bathroom. It scared me. Tony Phillips and Dave Parker were taking their drug tests at the urinals. Baseball finally began to require players to take random drug tests, but only after they had already been caught with drugs. I knew both of them were embarrassed when I walked in on them. They had come to our room to try to get some privacy. I knew Parker had drug problems, but I didn't know about Phillips.

I remember thinking back to what Brown said. These guys thought they were immune to everything, and once they tried it twice, they were hooked and couldn't get off the stuff. It was a sad time for baseball, and it went on far longer than it should have.

A lot of players never apologized for their drug use or even acted like they knew it was illegal. There was a pitcher on the Texas Rangers in 1981 who was giving his manager, Don Zimmer, a really hard time. Don was a throwback to what baseball was like in the fifties and sixties. We were in Anaheim, and when Don came to home plate before the game, he was talking about this player.

"I've been in this game for 32 years, and I've never seen anything like it," Zimmer said, shaking his head in disbelief. Of course he had our attention, so we said, "What happened, Don?"

He said a pitcher came into the locker room and was asking where he could get a small table. "What kind of table do you need?" a clubhouse attendant asked. The pitcher pointed to an empty room off the training room and said he wanted a table to put into that room.

Zimmer said he heard the conversation and asked what he needed the table for. The pitcher calmly said, "I need it to cut my cocaine on so I can do my lines." He acted like it was no big deal and was not embarrassed about the request at all.

After baseball finally seemed to get a little more control over the use of cocaine, a new problem developed—steroids. Again, I think the game's leaders are being very naïve in thinking they don't have a problem with players abusing steroids.

There have been claims by players like Jose Canseco and Ken Caminiti that most of the players in the majors are using steroids. I don't think the problem is that widespread, but I do think a lot of players are taking illegal supplements and enhancements.

All you have to do is look at the players to realize that they are doing something. You will never be able to tell me that Barry Bonds is not taking supplements. That's just my opinion. I have no proof, other than what I can see.

Bonds was called to testify before a grand jury in California in December 2003. The grand jury was called to investigate the use of steroids and other drugs by professional athletes. Major League Baseball is supposed to begin random testing for steroids in 2004, and it will be interesting to watch the results. A lot of people will make the argument that whatever a player wants to do to his own body is his own business, as long as it is legal, but I don't agree.

I will admit that I am a traditionalist, but baseball is about records and statistics, and steroids have changed that. Players who have taken steroids and set new records should have asterisks placed next to their names the way baseball did when Roger Maris broke Babe Ruth's single-season home-run record. Roger didn't do anything illegal; he just happened to play when the season had been expanded from 154 games to 162 games. That wasn't Roger's fault.

I know there are other differences in today's game. The parks are smaller, the pitching is not as good, the players are bigger and stronger because they can afford to work out year-round with personal trainers, and the equipment is better. Some pitchers in the big leagues now wouldn't have started in the Double A Texas League when I was coming up. But they are number one or number two starters because they are better than the rest of the pitchers on the team.

Why do players cheat? The answer is easy—the almighty dollar. A marginal player will do almost anything to stay in the major leagues, because he knows what it is going to mean to him financially. Players are willing to take the risk of getting caught, either with drugs or with throwing illegal pitches, because the financial reward is so great. If they can get away with it and are able to put big offensive numbers on the board or get one more hitter out, it's worth it. Every player is looking for an edge, and some think the only way they can get it is by doing something illegal.

But cheating is just one of the problems that the commissioner and the players association need to solve. It is by no means the only problem.

9

Juiced Balls and Strikes

My relationship with Bud Selig began long before he became the commissioner of baseball. He was the owner of the Milwaukee Brewers and was a good friend of umpire Bill Haller, who was a friend of mine. Bill nicknamed me Clyde, because we had worked David Clyde's first game in the major leagues in 1973. Clyde was just a few days out of high school. Clyde was called Baby Davie, and since my first name was Dave too, Haller started calling me that as well. That eventually changed to Baby Clyde, and then to just Clyde. Anytime Bill and I were in Milwaukee he would say, "Come on, Clyde, let's go see Selig."

Bud was always very friendly, and he loved to talk baseball. He is still that way, but the game has changed so much over the past few years that anytime Bud is talking now, he seems to be trying to solve a problem or put out a fire somewhere. It's amazing to think of all of the changes that have occurred in the game since Bud took over as commissioner —the wild-card, three divisions in each league, interleague play, playing games in Japan, Mexico, and Puerto Rico, and of course, canceling the 1994 World Series because of a players strike.

If you have to have an owner as commissioner, Bud is a good choice. He loves the game, but he is a consensus taker. That is what the owners want, and I don't think that has always helped him make the correct decision. He has had chances over the years to make some major decisions that would have affected the long-term future of the game, but in my opinion he always took the way out that pleased the owners. It is extremely hard to lead the owners; they don't want to be led. They are egotistical, they are wealthy, and they want everything done their way. They are not used to somebody telling them they can't do something. When they took away the power of the commissioner to act "in the best interests of baseball" it was a major mistake, because the commissioner should have that authority. The owners, however, were worried that that kind of authority would allow the commissioner to make decisions that they didn't like.

My biggest disappointment with Bud concerns what has happened with the umpires under the direction of Sandy Alderson. I thought when Sandy was hired from Oakland that it would be a positive move. He was portrayed as fair and honest, and he had always been friendly when he visited with the umpires while he was the general manager of the A's. I respected him and thought he had a chance to really improve the relationship with umpires. When he was hired, that was what he said was going to happen. He was very emphatic that nothing would be done without umpire input on every issue, that baseball wanted to build a good working relationship with the umpires and not have every issue be so confrontational. He billed it as a "new era for umpires and Major League Baseball." Despite that, in my opinion, the situation now is the worst it has ever been.

In the winter of 1999, a few months after Alderson joined the commissioner's office, all of the A.L. umpires were in New York for a meeting. Alderson wanted to meet with the whole staff. Instead the group selected umpires Tim Tschida, Jim Evans, and myself to join supervisor Marty Springstead and his assistant Phil Janssen at the meeting with Alderson; we would then report back to the group. During that meeting, if Sandy used the word *perception* once, he used it 15 times. He said umpires were perceived in a negative way, and what he wanted to do was create a different perception. He gave an example relating to Jose Canseco, who was with the A's when Alderson was their general manager. The A's knew he was perceived as a bad outfielder, so they decided to send him to the Arizona Instructional League for a couple of weeks to change that perception. They invited the press to watch his workouts and told them Canseco was working hard to become a better outfielder. Alderson said all he did was create the perception that Canseco was going to become a better outfielder—and the press believed it and wrote about it, doing exactly what Alderson had hoped for. I remember listening to the story and thinking, "Is the perception the only thing that's important to Alderson?"

Alderson was not yet officially in charge of the umpires, but it was coming. You could tell there was a contentious feeling at that meeting. He said he would like to set up a big meeting with all of the umpires from both leagues at a nice hotel during the winter, what companies today call a retreat. Marty Springstead was the supervisor of umpires for the American League, and he said he didn't think he had the budget to pay for a retreat like that. Alderson gave him a steel-eyed stare and said emphatically, "If I call a meeting, then by God we will have a meeting and I will have the money to pay for it." I'm certain it embarrassed Marty. Dick Butler, the supervisor of A.L. umpires, had told us many times over the years that Alderson was one of the worst general managers he ever dealt with regarding complaints about umpires, although most umpires thought Sandy was a decent guy.

While all this was going on in the commissioner's office, the umpires union, headed by Richie Phillips, was about to break up. Richie told the umpires that Alderson refused to negotiate. Because of that, Richie told us that he had a plan for all of the umpires to threaten Major League Baseball that we were going to resign if negotiations didn't begin in earnest. He had already written the resignation letters, and he presented them to us to sign. We all believed in what he said he was going to do—use them as a threat to get Alderson to begin negotiations for a new contract in earnest. In my mind (and those of many other umpires), that was his plan: threatening Alderson that the umpires were going to resign on September 2 if baseball did not start to negotiate immediately. I thought it was a good idea. The threat carried no risk, but did offer a great deal of reward. Because of their fear of the unknown, Major League Baseball would have no choice but to start negotiations.

What happened, however, was that Richie's threat turned into reality when he decided to fax all of the letters of resignation to the commissioner's office. I had no idea he was going to do that. Richie apparently believed those resignations could be rescinded at any time before September 2, but unfortunately he was wrong. They could be rescinded only if the commissioner's office or its representative, Alderson, allowed them to be rescinded. The employer has all the power when you have submitted a letter of resignation. Alderson capitalized on this opening.

When the union was breaking up, some of our more senior umpires were hoping the change would allow us to build a better relationship with the commissioner's office, more of a partnership instead of the controversial, adversarial relationship that had existed for years. Many of us thought that Richie had taken us as far as we could go. We appreciated everything he had done for us, but some thought it was time for a change. With the change in the commissioner's office as well, we thought the situation could work out well for everyone. Instead, Alderson was instrumental in hiring 22 new umpires to replace some of those who had resigned.

I quickly realized that our strategy had been a mistake on Richie's part, and I rescinded my resignation immediately. The relationship between the umpires and the commissioner's office was badly stained and continued to deteriorate over the next two years. Many umpires were upset about having to warn pitchers every time they threw a close pitch, and about the decision to grade umpires by pitch counts using the Ques-Tec system as an evaluating tool. (Ques-Tec is a computerized system that is supposed to measure whether a pitch is a ball or a strike. It then records the umpire's call and whether he called it "correctly" or not.) The tension reached the point that Larry Barnett resigned from his $75,000 a year job as supervisor. I would have been extremely upset if I had had to umpire games under those conditions, and I believed many others I worked with in the past would have felt the same way.

In my opinion, Alderson was determined to use the Ques-Tec system to create the perception that baseball was acknowledging the fact that there was a problem with the strike zone and that they were working to fix it. I also felt that baseball had a great opportunity to do it right but failed miserably. If they had wanted to do it right, they would have begun by *training* umpires to change the strike zone—in other words, they would have implemented a training program that would have given umpires the opportunity to perfect the changes Major League Baseball wanted to put in place. One of the biggest problems in baseball is that umpires receive little or no official training after they graduate from umpiring school in either the minors or the majors.

I hope baseball will work to find a way to keep up with technology and make it work for the umpires, who face so many challenges today—but the Ques-Tec system was not the right way to do it. Before the 2003 season, the new Ques-Tec system was installed at 10 ballparks around the majors without any scientific study as to its accuracy. The system reportedly was intended to help establish a standard strike zone and provide information to the umpires so they would know if they had called pitches correctly. In my opinion, it is a badly flawed system. The umpires hate it, the players hate it, and the bottom line is that it doesn't work. It is an embarrassment to Major League Baseball, but in my opinion they will not get rid of it because they are unwilling to admit their mistake.

When Alderson took office, Marty Springstead and Phil Janssen handed him a scientifically developed and tested umpire training and evaluation program. The program had been endorsed by college educators and the scientific community viewing it entirely from an educational and scientific viewpoint. Dr. Grant Secrest is a retired air force lieutenant colonel and a consultant for the military. He developed a system to train fighter pilots using simulators, and he was very interested in expanding this training and technology to the officiating profession. His plan would have worked well. It included a simulator that was similar to a golf training machine. It would have had the capabilities of a virtual reality device; theoretically, an umpire could put on a headset, dial up a particular pitcher, and see him actually pitching. An umpire could practice calling pitches in his living room. Dr. Secrest is one of the most intelligent men I have ever met, and he is extremely ethical. He knew the only way to create a better system was through *science* and *training*.

The problems with umpires today, however, run much deeper than the Ques-Tec system. The bottom line is no one seems to enjoy his job. When you come to the ballpark, you should be excited and ready to work a good game and have fun doing it. That isn't the case anymore because of all the rules, regulations, and intimidation forced on the umpires.

Umpires have a very difficult job, with a high degree of stress, and in my opinion, what baseball's leadership should be doing is creating a training program and instituting a scientifically proven system that is not only accurate but also private and secure—for umpires' use only. They need to create a system that will help umpires rather than intimidating them. Alderson never played the game or umpired, and that puts him in a tough position—having the task of instructing umpires in how to do their jobs when he never did it himself.

All of these changes would have made the job unbearable for me if I was still working. I respected the managers, coaches, and players, and I demanded the same from them. If an umpire wanted to ask a player how his new baby was doing or congratulate him on something he had accomplished, it didn't seem like a big deal or a problem to me. Saying "hi" to somebody before a game wasn't going to change the way I umpired or called a pitch or a play at first base. I could change my personable attitude in a hurry. If I had to eject somebody, I could do it in a New York minute, and frequently did, regardless of whether we had just had a conversation.

I always had the same attitude when I walked onto the field to start a game. I wanted to create a positive, energetic, and happy environment for my crew and the players and managers. I wanted everybody to know that our crew was glad to be there. I truly loved what I did for a living and tried to show my feelings every time I walked on the field. When an umpire doesn't enjoy his job, I think it shows in his attitude and performance. I never wanted to start a game mad or upset. It goes back to the lessons I learned in the minor leagues—a great percentage of being a good umpire is the ability to handle people. A good umpire has to have good people skills. You can be a good technical umpire, getting the ball-strike, fair-foul, safe-out calls right, but still be considered a mediocre umpire if you don't know how to handle people and situations.

In my opinion, umpires are going onto the field feeling intimidated by the Ques-Tec system, and you can't umpire that way. If an umpire wants to talk to the third baseman, so be it, as long as he is in position to make a call. An umpire should work hard, have fun, and always act professionally.

When I look back on it, Ron Luciano was probably wrong in the way he umpired, even though I enjoyed our time together. His reputation as an entertainer was not the kind of image an umpire should portray. But by the same token, the umpire's role shouldn't be so rigid that he can't talk to another umpire or a coach or player. Managers, coaches, and players are all "employees" of the same "company": *baseball.* Baseball is a game played and officiated by human beings— and we all make mistakes. Therefore, we need to have that mutual respect for our profession. Having a good relationship with the people you are working with helps build that trust and credibility that an umpire must have to earn the benefit of the doubt and do a good job.

I have played golf with many players and coaches in charity tournaments, and I consider most of them friends. If I walk into a bar or restaurant and see a player or manager I know, I am going to say hello and I might even buy them a drink. However, I never made any formal plans to meet a player, coach, or manager off the field—I was friendly and never rude, but I tried to always be professional.

One of the best umpires I ever worked with was Steve Palermo. He and I were partners for 10 years. Steve had style, charisma, showmanship, personality, and guts. He would talk, laugh, and have fun, but by God he ran his game every day, and the players and managers respected him. We worked hard, had fun, and acted like professionals. That should be the goal of every umpire. An umpire must be serious, but should never allow himself to become overly aggressive, argumentative, lackadaisical, or complacent.

The relationship between umpires and the league offices has never been good, but it was starting to improve over the years. What worries me the most about the current situation is that I see all of that progress being eliminated if some changes don't occur soon.

When I broke into the major leagues in 1971, my salary was $10,000 a year. We had a union, and Jack Reynolds, a lawyer from Chicago, was our representative. He was nice enough, but he really didn't have the support he needed or the desire to force baseball into taking better care of the umpires. He lasted for a couple of years, and then we fired him and hired John Cifelli.

John was a little more aggressive, and we made some small gains during his term. In 1971, in addition to our salary, umpires were making $40 a day meal money. He got that increased to $52, but that was supposed to cover all of our expenses, including the hotel, trips to and from the ballpark, trips to and from the airport, clubhouse tips, cleaning, and of course, food. Although the dollar went much further 30 years ago, that amount still couldn't possibly cover our expenses. Cifelli lasted until 1978, when he was fired and replaced by Richie Phillips.

I was the only A.L. umpire involved in hiring Richie. We interviewed him extensively at the Waldorf Astoria in New York and tried to find out as much about him as we could. We talked about the history of our previous representatives and their negotiations with Major League Baseball, and I remember saying to him, "We've had a guy [Reynolds] who threatened Major League Baseball that he had a gun, and another guy [Cifelli] who said he had a gun and showed it, but we've never had anybody who showed the gun, threatened, and then pulled the trigger."

Richie looked me in the eye and said, "Dave, if you guys show me the strength I need and we work together, I will not only show you the gun but also pull the trigger and blow their f****** heads off." He was immediately my choice for the job.

The umpires were so upset by their situation in the late seventies that we all rallied behind Richie and went out on strike at the start of the 1979 season. We all believed we were being mistreated and grossly underpaid. Because we didn't make much money to begin with, a lot of the umpires were absolutely devastated financially by the strike, but we stuck together. Baseball threatened to fire us three times, but we stayed on strike for six weeks.

It was difficult, costly, and embarrassing to go out and picket the stadiums, but we did it because we wanted people to know what was happening. We heard a lot of negative comments, but we also were determined to stick it out, because we knew we were right. We gained a lot of support and respect when Major League Baseball realized that not just anyone who walked in off the street could do our jobs. My wife, Sharon, was worried that I was going to lose my job, but I knew we had one big intangible working in our favor: *credibility.*

One day we were picketing in Pittsburgh—a very tough pro-union town because of the steelworkers—and union members were informing everybody coming into the stadium that the umpires were on strike. A broadcaster, Milo Hamilton, drove up in his car and was stopped by a steelworker. I doubt the man knew Milo was a broadcaster; he politely asked if Milo was aware that the umpires were on strike and that scab umpires were working the game. Milo got mad and told the man to get out of his way. Before they finally let his car pass, this tough, mean steelworker snapped the radio antenna off Milo's car and nonchalantly flipped it on the hood of the car. The steelworkers didn't like his sarcastic attitude. We found out after the game that Milo's car somehow had four flat tires. The situation was starting to get nasty.

I remember a big rally we organized in Detroit, a major union town. We decided to hold a press conference to demonstrate that the other union leaders were supporting us. Richie came in for the news conference, and a lot of press people were there. Unfortunately, only one union executive showed up, and that didn't look too impressive.

Richie and I and the other umpires who were there went into a side room and decided we had to make this look better. Most of the press there knew the American League umpires but not the N.L. guys. We decided to create a perception by using some lesser known N.L. umpires as union executive imposters. Dutch Rennert became the head of the Teamsters. I believe Joe West was the autoworkers representative. Richie drilled them about how to act and what to say.

The next morning, we went to Tiger Stadium to picket. All of the groundskeepers were friends of ours, and they came outside to join us on the picket line. They were not happy about their contract situation either, but they knew they would be fired if they were not back in the stadium by noon because of their no-strike clause. We understood, but of course the Tigers didn't know they were planning to be back in time to get the field ready to play the game. Richie had a local bar open up at 7:00 A.M. and paid for all the drinks for the groundskeepers. As you can imagine, that made them extremely happy.

Jim Campbell was the general manager of the Tigers, and he was a very tough and harsh individual, all business, but considered a fair guy. The field was still covered with the tarp as the teams were getting ready to warm up. The head of stadium operations for the Tigers came out to threaten the ground crew that he would fire them if they didn't go back in the stadium. I was the most senior umpire there, so I told him that we needed to talk to Campbell. We were bluffing, of course, because we knew the groundskeepers were going to be in the stadium in time for the game, but the Tigers didn't know that.

Finally, Campbell sent word out for me to come into the stadium and he would talk to me on the phone. "Dave, you've got to get this f****** tarp off the field," he pleaded. "The grass is burning up."

"Jim, I would love to do that, but we've got to get a paycheck, too," I said. We wanted him to call Lee MacPhail and tell him how ridiculous this situation was. I made him promise to call MacPhail, and said if he would do that, I would encourage the ground crew to go back. He promised that he would call MacPhail and do what he could to help us. It made us look good to have the groundskeepers come back into the stadium, but in reality it was just a big bluff.

Campbell was true to his word and called MacPhail, and soon after that we got the strike resolved. It had taken me five years in the major leagues to see my salary go from $10,000 a year to $20,000, and I shot right through the

$30,000s and it just kept on going. I never dreamed as a kid coming to the major leagues that I would make the kind of money I eventually made. Richie Phillips deserves to be congratulated because until we had those problems with the resignations, which cost him his job, he was tremendous.

Almost better than the salary raise, however, was the fact that we came out of the strike with vacation time during the season. We didn't even ask for it. What happened was, for baseball to get umpires to cross our picket lines and work, they had to guarantee them three-year contracts and promised they would not be fired if the regular umpires came back to work. I never had a three-year contract in my entire career. Because of that, however, baseball had all of these extra guys that had to be paid and had to work for three years, so they said, "Oh, by the way, we want to give you all two-week vacations."

Before that, the only time off an umpire had during the season was the three days at the All-Star break. Many umpires didn't think the vacation time was a big deal, but it was huge to me. I still think it was probably the greatest thing we ever achieved in negotiations, and we didn't even ask for it. It really helps if you are able to get away from the game for a while, recharge your batteries, and come back refreshed.

The players and managers were among the happiest people to have the regular umpires back. The replacement umpires were truck drivers or teachers, or they worked for the street department by day and were working major league games at night. The players knew their performance was being impacted by the strike, and they didn't want their success or failure to be determined by a fireman or a fry cook. It was not a good situation for anybody involved. I always knew we would win because what we had was something the replacements never had—*credibility*.

During the strike, Bill Haller and I were sitting in the lobby of the Hilton Hotel in Chicago, waiting to go out and picket at Comiskey Park, when Nestor Chylak joined our conversation. Nestor had a stroke in 1978 and was not able to umpire anymore, so they had made him a supervisor. During the strike, his job was to go around and talk to the managers and urge them to take it easy on the new umpires.

Bill had been raised in Joliet, Illinois, and his father, Rod, was a steelworker. Evidently, they had gone on strike for a long time when Bill was a young boy, and it had been a really nasty situation for his family. Bill had been raised in that environment, a union atmosphere. He was a real soft-spoken guy, until he got mad; then you had better watch out.

We were sitting in the lobby, and Bill was smoking his pipe, looking very distinguished. Nestor came up to us, and while we were talking, another man walked up. Nestor introduced us to him. His name was Dick Nelson, and he was one of the new umpires. As soon as Nestor finished talking, Bill jumped up from the sofa and started yelling.

"You scab. You no-good SOB," Haller screamed. "Get away from me, you scab." People were staring at him, but Bill didn't care. Nelson took off running. I was laughing hysterically, but Bill was serious. As soon as Nelson left, Bill sat back down and put his pipe back in his mouth as if nothing had happened.

A few of the umpires who were hired when we were on strike stayed in the game for years. They were never allowed into the union, they were forced to make their own travel and hotel arrangements, and the other umpires never had anything to do with them. Some umpires wouldn't even talk to them when they were on the field, but I never did that. I would not socialize with any of those men off the field, but on the field I didn't want my personal feelings to ever interfere with our crew's ability to perform our job in a professional manner. One of the lessons my dad taught me is that an umpire is only as strong as his partner. If your partner is in trouble, so are you. I tried to live by that advice throughout my entire career.

Two of those replacement umpires who survived in the game for many years were John Shulock and Darryl Cousins, and both were good umpires and good guys.

Of course, there were times when umpires didn't talk to each other, on the field or off, and it had nothing to do with union issues.

My first year in the majors, working with Larry Napp as our crew chief, was spent with Jerry Neudecker and Russ Goetz. Neither Jerry nor Russ cared for Napp, which was bad enough for a rookie like me; but by the middle of the year, Jerry and Russ were not speaking to each other either.

We had a game in Boston—the same game in which I ejected Reggie Jackson—when Neudecker and Napp got into it. Neudecker had the plate, and Napp was at third. The game was on national television, which in 1971 was a big deal. There was a question about whether a hitter had checked his swing, and Dick Williams came out of the dugout to ask Neudecker to check with Napp. Neudecker had said he had not swung. The rule at the time was that an umpire was not required to ask another umpire if a batter

COMISKEY PARK

Here I'm turning over Albert Belle's bat to clubhouse attendant Vinny Fresso during a game in 1994, setting off one of the league's bigger scandals in recent memory. The bat, suspected of being corked, was stolen from my locker during the game and replaced with one of Belle's teammates' "clean" bats. Years later I was finally able to confirm my suspicions about who the "burglar" had been.

The Cleveland Indians nicknamed our umpiring crew "DiMuro's Destroyers" after we worked a number of problematic games involving them and their manager, Frank Robinson, at the start of the 1976 season. Here, as Robinson pleads with crew chief Lou DiMuro, I have to come all the way out to short center field from behind the plate to let Frank know once and for all that he'd been ejected.

I was involved in another famous illegal bat incident besides the one with Belle: the George Brett pine tar game in 1983. I thought Yankees manager Billy Martin (No. 1) was going to faint when I pulled out an affidavit to squelch his argument during the continuation of this controversial game.

A safe call on a close play at the plate, with Brewers Hall of Famer Robin Yount beating the tag by Yankees catcher Rick Cerone.

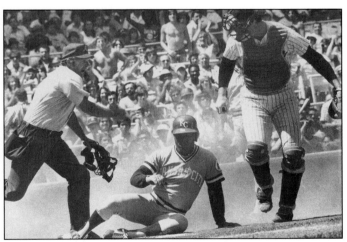

Another close play at the plate, this time with Kansas City's Hal McRae getting called out. Years later, when McRae was managing the Royals, I once threatened to have the cops come down and remove him from the field because he wouldn't go back to the dugout after an argument.

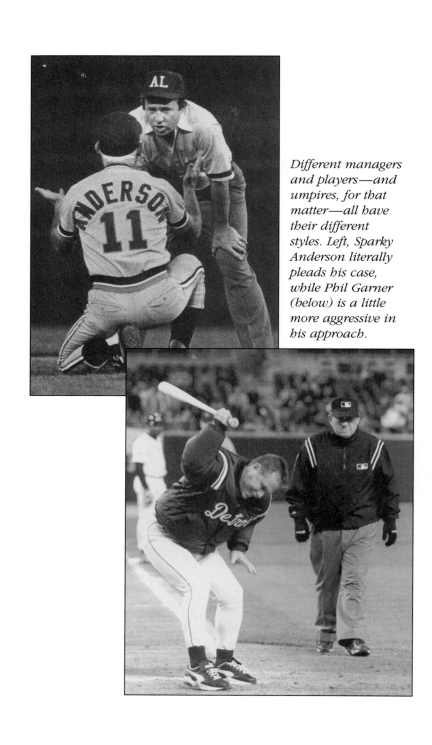

Different managers and players—and umpires, for that matter—all have their different styles. Left, Sparky Anderson literally pleads his case, while Phil Garner (below) is a little more aggressive in his approach.

The umpires went on strike for six weeks during the 1979 season. Here, Bruce Froemming and Don Denkinger are talking with Brewers owner and current commissioner Bud Selig before picketing outside County Stadium in Milwaukee.

Here I'm just cooling off in front of the blower (see my hat) in Minnesota during the 1987 World Series, one of four World Series that I worked. There was a controversy at the time about whether the blowers were being turned on and off during the games.

My beautiful wife—and former high school sweetheart—Sharon.

Here I am with my son, Randy, before the start of a game. I knew I had at least one fan in the stands pulling for me that day.

My three children (from left): Kim, Randy, and Jill.

It's a difficult, thankless, sometimes lonely or cold job, but I wouldn't trade my 32 years as a big-league umpire for anything in the world.

had swung. After a long argument, Neudecker finally agreed to check and Napp overruled him and said he had swung. Jerry was livid after the game because Napp had embarrassed him and shown him up on national television.

About three months later, the same play happened again, in reverse, and this time Neudecker overruled Napp. The team started screaming, and poor Jerry had to eject two players. He couldn't win. Jerry and Napp got into arguments before the game, and Jerry and Russ got into such big disagreements I don't think they spoke to each other from June until the end of the season.

We had a doubleheader in Anaheim, and each of them had the plate for one game. Goetz went to the ballpark four hours early to rub up his half of the baseballs so he wouldn't have to sit there and do it at the same time Jerry was rubbing up his game balls. The next day, when we were going to the park, Jerry was driving, and Russ and I were in the backseat. The radio was on, coming out of the rear speakers, and Goetz asked if Jerry would please turn the radio down. Jerry ignored him and continued to let the radio blare.

We finished the game, and Goetz took a really quick shower, got dressed, got the car keys, and went out to the car to wait. Jerry was determined to let him sit, so he took his sweet time getting ready. Finally, we went to the car, and Goetz was sitting behind the wheel. We didn't say anything, just got in the car. Goetz started the car, and I thought the windows were going to blow out. The radio was on full blast. It was as loud as you can imagine. He started to drive back to the hotel and now Jerry was screaming at Goetz to turn the *goddamn* radio down. I was laughing so hard tears were rolling down my face. Unfortunately, we had to stop at a train crossing, and people looked at us like we were crazy. Goetz never turned it down either. Napp never said a word; he just shook his head in disbelief.

We were in New York the day before the All-Star break. One thing Goetz had done was to keep every stat for every game we had worked that year—the score, time of game, ejections, pitches, balls, strikes, everything. He had obviously spent a tremendous amount of time compiling that vast amount of information for us. As we got into a cab to go to Yankee Stadium, the three of us were sitting in the backseat. I was in the middle, as usual for a rookie. Everybody was happy because we were going home for three days.

We didn't know Goetz had kept all of this information, but he started handing it out to us like a gift. He was proud of it. As soon as he handed it to Jerry, Jerry ripped it in half and threw it on the floor. Again, all I could do was laugh. It really was a sad situation, but it was just so funny to see these grown men acting like this. We came back after the All-Star break and they never spoke for the rest of the year, which made it very difficult for me as a rookie umpire. If I spoke to one, the other got mad.

My memories from that season were why I was determined not to let the fact that I didn't care for some umpires personally, or disagreed with their actions when it came to union activities, take away from our professionalism on the field. There were umpires who were vicious about it. I never went out of my way to be involved with the nonunion guys, but I always came into their arguments and helped them on the field because it's what a partner and a crew chief is supposed to do. The worst thing about it was that some of those umpires stayed in the league for a long time, never paid a dime in union dues, and received all of the same benefits the rest of us did. I don't blame them—they wanted to join the union, they wanted to pay their dues, but the union wouldn't allow them to join, which I thought was a mistake.

One of the best things that has happened to the umpires in recent years was combining the A.L. and N.L. staffs into one staff. Some N.L. umpires were against it, and I think the main reason is that the American League traditionally plays longer games because of the designated hitter. You have more runs, more runners running the bases, more pitches to call, and more pitching changes in the middle of the inning because you can't pinch hit for the pitcher. None of that is the umpire's fault. However, it creates more pressure for an umpire because any time you have more things to call there are obviously more chances for making a mistake.

One of the biggest misconceptions in the game has been that there is a difference in the strike zones between umpires who were A.L. umpires and the umpires who came up in the N.L. That indeed used to be the case when the American League umpires were required to wear the big outside chest protector. A.L. umpires called a higher strike because they couldn't get low enough to call such a low pitch.

As soon as the A.L. let us get rid of that outside protector, I was the first to change to the inside one, along with Don Denkinger. Jim Evans, Richie Garcia, and others soon followed. My old partner, Jerry Neudecker, was the last umpire to use the outside protector, the day before Phil Niekro won his 300th career game in Toronto.

All of the umpires strikes, whether they have lasted only a few days or six weeks, as in 1979, created bad feelings between the owners and the umpires union. The strikes also brought about negative press coverage, which baseball officials cannot stand, but it in no way compared to the number of negative stories that appeared each time the players went on strike.

There were two major strikes by the players during my career, in 1981 and 1994. The strike in 1981 came in the middle of the season and lasted for two months. Of course, the owners caved in, as they have always done, and gave the players union exactly what they had asked for before they went on strike. I enjoyed the time off because I was home with my family in June, July, and August and still got paid.

The worst strike was the walkout in 1994, which prompted Selig to call off the World Series. We were in Oakland the day before the strike was supposed to begin, and nobody was telling us anything. The A's were playing Seattle, and Tim McClelland was working the plate. Dan Wilson, the Mariners' catcher, was their player rep, and Tim casually asked him what was going on.

"It's over. We're done," Wilson told him. "When this game is over, we're done. There will be no baseball tomorrow or for some time." He was right, even though I don't think anybody thought when the strike began that it would not be over in a couple of weeks.

I had been worried because my daughter Kim was going to be married in September and I didn't know how I was going to get a week off to come home and prepare for the wedding. It turned out I was home the whole time, and for my daughter Jill's wedding in November as well. A strike year, and both my girls got married—it must have been umpire's luck. Now I have two great sons-in-law and five grandchildren, so it was *really* good luck.

What amazed me was that the next spring, the strike still had not been resolved, and baseball came up with the idea of using replacement players. They actually played spring-training games and were on the verge of opening the regular season with them when Sparky Anderson came out and said he would not manage the replacement players, and the owners finally caved in again.

For baseball to cancel the World Series and come out of the strike with nothing was absolutely ridiculous. If you are going to cancel the World Series over the issues, by God you better come back with something. They should have just shut down for the entire season the next year if that was what it took. Instead, the players again came back with almost the same exact basic agreement as they had before.

I never understood what people meant when they said all of the real baseball people had left the game, but I have it figured out now. People like Charlie Finley, Bill Veeck, Calvin Griffith, John Fetzer, Walter O'Malley, Horace Stoneham, and Tom Yawkey were the true baseball people. They were big businessmen too, but they were fans. They loved the game. It was their life. Now, the money is so great that owners cannot focus entirely on the game anymore. Teams are owned by corporations or conglomerates, and their biggest concern is the bottom line, because they know they will have to answer to the stockholders if they lose money.

There is no doubt the game has changed, and not necessarily for the better. An umpire's goal, however, has remained the same—to walk out on that field and officiate the game as fairly as possible, and hope when the game is over, he can walk back into the dressing room without any controversy, because that means he has done his job and has done it well.

As everybody knows, however, that isn't always what happens.

10

Umpires' Nightmares

When baseball fans in St. Louis believe an umpire has missed a call, the first name that comes to mind is Don Denkinger. It's a shame, because Don was a very good umpire. I worked on his crew for two years and worked other games with him as well. He just was in the wrong place at the wrong time, a victim of umpire's luck.

Don was working first base during Game 6 of the 1985 World Series between the Cardinals and the Royals. He was the crew chief, meaning he also worked home plate during the first game and would have the plate again if there was a seventh game. The Cardinals thought they were on the verge of winning the game in the bottom of the ninth inning, when the Royals' Jorge Orta hit a ground ball to Cardinals first baseman Jack Clark.

Todd Worrell was the pitcher, and he came over to first to take the throw from Clark. Don was in position to make the call, and he ruled that Orta was safe, that either Worrell was off the base or Orta beat the throw. The Cardinals argued, but to no avail—the call stood. The instant replays immediately showed that Don had missed the call.

The Royals, as umpire's luck would have it, capitalized on the opening and scored two runs to win the game, tie the series, and force the seventh and deciding game the next night.

I was not on the crew for that particular World Series, but I was watching the game while attending a wedding reception. I saw the play on one of the monitors. As soon as I saw what had happened, we decided to leave. I know exactly what would have happened had we not left as quickly as we did—everybody there would have been talking to me, asking my opinion, wanting to know why Don had missed the call.

We lived only five minutes from where the reception was being held, so we were home before the game was over. When Kansas City won, I felt terrible for Don and his wife, Gail, who had just been at my house the day before. They were driving back and forth from Kansas City to St. Louis during the Series.

I was also very concerned about their three daughters, who were at their home in Iowa, staying with their grandmother. I knew those girls and their grandmother well. I had watched them grow up during our time together each spring. I knew they were watching the game on television and had heard all the comments about their dad and would be upset, so I picked up the phone and called them.

One of the girls answered, and she was crying. She asked who it was, and I told her, and she started crying even harder. "Oh, Davey," she said, "they are being so mean to my dad."

I got Gail's mom, Margaret, on the phone, and she said they were getting terrible phone calls from people threatening to blow up their house, people saying they didn't want them living in their town—unimaginable stuff. I told the girls, "Listen, your dad is a great umpire. Don't worry about this." I knew what Don had to be going through at the stadium, but I also really felt sorry for his girls and family because they certainly had nothing to do with the play in Kansas City. Don had an excellent reputation in his home town, and the girls were really upset. I knew my kids would have reacted the same way, and I know I was thinking about how Kim and Jill would have felt when I made that call.

Learning from Don's experience, I honestly think the most important game of the World Series for an umpire is the sixth game. The reason is, you have got to get to the seventh game cleanly, without an incident, or you are going to have problems even before the seventh game starts. You can't have a gigantic controversy at first base in Game 6 or it will carry over to the seventh game. Unfortunately, Don didn't have that luxury.

If the Cardinals had won the seventh game, that play at first base would have been forgotten very quickly; it would have been a nonissue. When the Royals pounded the Cardinals 11–0, however, with Whitey Herzog and Joaquin Andujar being ejected from the game by Don, it became an even bigger issue.

If that same play had happened on a July night in Cleveland, nobody would have noticed it. But now, the Denkinger name is still taken in vain in St. Louis at least 25 times a year. Other umpires didn't believe me when I told them that, so I started cutting out the articles from the newspaper and sending them to them. If a sewer main breaks or there is a bad storm or anything negative happens in St. Louis, somebody will associate it with Don—it doesn't even have to be about sports.

Don, to his credit, admitted later when he saw the replay that he had missed the call. There wasn't anything that could be done about it at that point, however, except hope that it never happened again.

It was a television replay that almost got me into trouble on a play two years later when I was working the plate in the seventh game of the 1987 World Series between the Cardinals and the Minnesota Twins.

It was a fun Series, and our crew was having a good Series. At the time, it became the only World Series in history in which the home team won every game. I really think it was one of the few times in my career when the opposing team had a tremendous disadvantage playing the Twins, especially a National League team that had never played in the Metrodome. It is probably the worst place ever to play a baseball game. Cleveland's old stadium was bad and there are and were a lot of other miserable stadiums, but no place is as bad as the Metrodome. It is unfortunate because Minneapolis is a beautiful city, and for them to build a stadium like that for baseball was absolutely ridiculous. It was built for football, and bad weather, and it is so bad that even the people sitting behind home plate are sitting at an angle, instead of looking directly at the plate.

The stadium gave the Twins a definite advantage, but the Cardinals still got to a seventh game. In the middle of that game, Don Baylor was trying to score on a hit to the outfield. Steve Lake was the catcher for the Cardinals, and he got the ball well before Baylor got to the plate. I have a five-picture sequence of the play in my den, and in the first three pictures, Lake has the ball and Baylor isn't even in the picture yet.

Looking back on it, I know exactly what happened. Lake had the ball for so long that he expected Baylor would try to crash into him and knock the ball loose, so he was bracing himself for the collision. Instead, Baylor came in with a normal slide as if to say, "Go ahead and tag me. I know I'm out."

It was an easy call. Baylor was out and nobody said anything. It was the third out of the inning, so I walked back toward the stands to wait while the two teams changed sides. About two minutes later, all of a sudden everybody in the stadium started booing. Nobody on the field knew what they were booing about. The play had been over for a long time—then I figured it out.

When the television broadcast came back from the commercials between innings, they showed the replay. The fans in the stands were watching it on television monitors. The announcers, Al Michaels, Jim Palmer, and Tim McCarver, said that Baylor was never tagged and could have been called safe. All I can say about that play is if I had called Baylor safe, there would have been several ejections because of the arguments it would have caused. I know Herzog and Lake would have been ejected for sure, and maybe others as well.

It was generally accepted practice in baseball that if a ball beats a runner, he is going to be called out. If the ball beats the runner, he is expecting to be called out. That has changed a little over the years, but it still happens that way more times than not. In this case, the ball so clearly beat Baylor to the plate that for me to call him safe would have been contrary to everything I had been taught as an umpire. If it was the wrong call, how come there were no arguments from the Twins?

The worst part about that call for me was that when I got home to St. Louis the next night, I read in the newspaper that a man in Milwaukee had been watching the game on television and had gotten so upset by the call that he had suffered a heart attack and died. I felt terrible, and I called information and tracked down the funeral home in Milwaukee that was handling the man's arrangements.

I eventually got the man's son on the phone and explained who I was and why I was calling. The man was very polite and appreciative that I had called. He said the newspaper had blown that out of proportion. He said he was with his father at the time, and he was watching the game, but the call had nothing to do with his fatal heart attack. I felt better after that.

Umpires are always worried about instant replays, and they shouldn't be, because all of the replays over the years have shown how great the umpires are about getting the calls right. So much of the replay depends on the angle of the camera and the positioning of the players, and sometimes you can't see or hear the ball hitting the glove if the camera is focusing on the base.

I was working the 1985 American League playoffs between Toronto and Kansas City when we had a play that was so close even the announcers couldn't tell what to call it. Frank White of the Royals hit a low line drive to center field, and

Lloyd Moseby, the center fielder for Toronto, either caught it or trapped it. Ted Hendry was working second base, and he went out to center to make the call, but he couldn't tell. Instead, he looked at me, working the right-field line, and pointed for me to make the call.

I was 150 feet away, but I immediately said no catch, indicating that Moseby had trapped it. There was no doubt in my mind that I had made the right call. The angry Toronto fans of course didn't agree and were mad, and they started throwing money at me on the field. I tried to ignore it at first, but then I made the mistake of picking up a few coins. Then the fans really showered me. I guess I was hoping to get enough to pay my hotel bill. I called time and went in and told league president Bobby Brown to have an announcement made for the fans to stop throwing items on the field. I always wanted to thank the fans for giving me the money to pay my toll to the airport after the game, however. I found out later that Darryl Cousins, who was working the left-field line, had also signaled no catch at the same time I did, but nobody had seen him. It became a moot point anyway when Toronto came back and won the game. This time umpire's luck worked in my favor.

Bob Costas was doing the game for NBC, and he told me later he and the other announcers and staff watched the replay 25 times and they were split on whether or not they thought it was a catch. That proves that even with improved technology, it would be hard for television to ever play a roll in making calls.

I was working a game in Chicago when Reggie Jackson was called out on strikes on a close pitch. Greg Kosc was the home-plate umpire, and when they showed the replay on the scoreboard, Reggie stood at the plate and pointed to the scoreboard. Greg almost ejected him because of the replay, even though clubs had been instructed not to show replays. Tony LaRussa was managing the White Sox, and he shrugged his shoulders because he was also upset. I went into the dugout and tried to call the owner, Jerry Reinsdorf, on the phone. He wasn't at the game, but they connected me to his partner, Eddie Einhorn. I don't know if he knew I was working the game or not because he said jovially, "Hey, Davey, good to hear from you. Where are you? What are you doing?"

I said, "Eddie, I'm down here in the goddamn dugout." I looked up to the club-box level and saw him standing there, and I waved. "I want to tell you right now I don't want to see any more replays on the board." Eddie agreed and said he was upset too, and it turned out he fired the guy who had run the replay on the board.

We had the same thing happen in Oakland one time with a replay, and after the game the A's president, Roy Eisenhardt, was waiting in our dressing room. He said how embarrassed and sorry he was that it had happened, and he promised us it would never happen again.

When the replays first came into popularity, there was a learning process about which plays to show and which not to show. The technology at the time was not nearly as good as it is now, and the picture quality in many cases was poor. It was black and white, not color, and you had a hard time seeing the screen during day games. I know teams wanted to show the replays because they were trying to give fans more for their dollar, but it can be a scary situation.

It is one thing to show a replay on television, because that fan usually isn't sitting where he can throw a beer bottle on the field or come onto the field himself. A fan sitting at the game having a beer or two is going to see what he wants to see on the replay and is going to be convinced the umpire blew the call, if it went against his team. He sees what he wants to see. Umpires don't want anything to happen that could incite a riot in the stands.

Sometimes, however, you don't need a replay to know you have missed a call.

In my second year, I was working third base during a Sunday afternoon game at Fenway Park. The Red Sox were playing the Twins, and Harmon Killebrew hit a rocket down the left-field line. Carl Yastrzemski was in left field for Boston. I could tell it was going to hit close to the line, so I pivoted and focused my attention on the wall, where there is a yellow stripe that runs up the Green Monster to the start of the foul pole. I focused on that, and I saw the ball hit right in the middle of that line, so I signaled that it was a fair ball.

I had no more made the call when Yastrzemski jumped in the air and came running toward me. Luis Aparicio and Rico Petrocelli were pointing at the wall and screaming at me as well. Eddie Kasko came running out of the Boston dugout.

Before he could say anything, I said, "The ball hit the yellow line." Everybody was pointing, and finally I noticed that everybody was looking at the ground, but I could not imagine what they were looking for. Nobody got ejected, and we resumed and then finished the game.

Back in the dressing room, I said to Jim Evans, who had worked the plate, "I can't believe they made such a big deal about that play. Did you see it the same way I did?" He told me no, he thought it was a foul ball.

We went back and forth replaying the play. I said, "Did you see the ball hit the yellow line?" Jim didn't know what yellow line I was talking about—the foul line is white, he said. That's when I figured out what had happened. Evidently I was so focused on the wall that I did not see the ball first hit the ground in foul territory. It then hit the side wall and bounced back and hit the far wall—the wall I had been watching the whole time. It was definitely a mistake on my part, watching the wall, and it was a learning experience I tried to use for the rest of my career—watch the ball, not the wall.

Fenway has a lot of nooks and crannies, and the fans were allowed to wear white shirts in the center-field stands, making it a very difficult place to umpire. But it was one of my favorite parks. All you had to do was walk into the ballpark and you could not help but think about all of the history that had occurred there, from Babe Ruth's days to Ted Williams', and much more. It is a special place.

Evans and I were involved in another "was it fair or foul" play during the 1982 World Series between St. Louis and Milwaukee.

It was Game 3, in Milwaukee. Jim was working third base and I was at first. Silent George Hendrick hit a ball down the third-base line, and Jim threw his arms up in the air, which to me signaled that it was a foul ball. I immediately threw my arms up as well, but Paul Molitor fielded the ball and threw to Cecil Cooper at first. It was going to be a bang-bang play, but I didn't even think about calling Hendrick out or safe because I knew Jimmy had called it a foul ball. There was no call for me to make.

All of sudden, after Hendrick passed first, Evans came running toward me: "I called that ball fair," he said. I thought he was kidding me, but he was serious. John Kibler was working the plate, and he had to make the call at first since I hadn't been concentrating on the play. Fortunately, Kibler saw the play and he said Hendrick was clearly safe.

Naturally, the Brewers' manager, Harvey Kuenn, came out, but he didn't put up too much of an argument, and luckily the play didn't figure into the outcome of the game. His argument ended when Silent George, who never talked to the media, actually spoke. "Har-veeeey," he said very slowly, "you know I was safe."

After the game, I had to get this cleared up with Evans, who was then and still is today a very close friend. When we got into the dressing room I nicely said to him, "Did you know you called the ball foul?"

"I don't know what you saw," he said, "but I called it fair the whole time." He was convinced he had not raised his arms up in the air.

When I told Jim he had raised his arms, he said he had not. I knew we weren't going to agree, so I let it go. The next morning, when I opened the door of my hotel room, the newspaper was sitting on the floor. On the front page was a big photo of Jim with his arms raised—the universal sign for a foul ball. I was happy to realize that I was not going blind.

Evans and I worked together in our early years in the majors under Nestor Chylak, and I never will forget one day when Chylak missed a call and tried to blame Jim for his mistake. It was in New York, and Ralph Houk came out to argue. Chylak didn't like managers coming out to argue with him, because it obviously embarrassed him. Dick Butler, our supervisor, also happened to be at the game, and he came into our dressing room after the game. Butler was never going to criticize Chylak, or even ask him about it, because Chylak was one of his senior umpires. But instead of waiting to see what Butler said to him, Nestor started yelling at Evans.

"Jimmy, what have I told you all year?" he yelled. "When you've missed a play, haven't I told you time and time again that you were too close to the play? Haven't I preached to you all year about that?" There was no need for this tirade; Chylak was doing it solely to impress Butler, take the blame off himself, and pick on the rookie.

Finally Nestor stopped yelling, turned real quick so Butler was behind him, and said in a very soft, quiet voice, "And what did I do today?" He knew he had done exactly what he had been preaching against all year.

It is one of the unwritten rules of the game that an umpire is going to miss a play once in a while. Umpires aren't robots, so they are not going to be 100 percent accurate. You just hope when you do miss a call, it doesn't turn out to be at a crucial time, as it was with Don Denkinger, or that it doesn't decide the game the wrong way. Umpire's luck, however, usually dictates that it happens just the way you don't want it to.

I was working second base in Oakland, on June 30, 1995, and the A's were playing Anaheim. The Angels were leading 5–4 going into the bottom of the ninth inning. A ball was hit to right field, and I slipped while I was moving toward second to get in position to make the call if there was a play. I didn't think there was going to be a play at second, because the ball looked like it would be a sure double.

Tim Salmon got to the ball quickly and made an unbelievable throw. He had a rifle for an arm, and he threw the ball to second. I called the runner safe, but as soon as I finished making the call I thought I was wrong.

It could have been the first out of the inning, but instead Oakland loaded the bases with two outs and Mark McGwire coming up to bat. I was hoping against hope that he would make an out, but of course he didn't. He hit a monster shot for a grand slam that gave Oakland an 8–5 win. I didn't even turn around to watch the ball. If I could have crawled under second base I would have.

Marcel Lachemann was managing the Angels, and he was good about it the next day, but I had a difficult time going to sleep that night. Umpires care deeply, and we hate to be wrong.

Durwood Merrill told me a story about when he missed a play while he was working in the Texas League. Bobby Bragan was the league president, and he called Durwood into his office to talk about it. Bragan asked him to explain the entire play, and then in his Texas drawl he said, "Now, Dur-wooood, if you had the chance to do it over again, would you call it the same way?"

Durwood answered very emphatically that if he had to do it over again right then, he would call the play exactly the same way, to which Bragan replied, "Then Dur-wooood, you would have f***** it up twice." Bragan was notorious with umpires as a minor league manager, but he was truly one of the best league presidents an umpire could have when it came to getting the league's support.

What an umpire doesn't want is to become involved in a play. That happened to me one day in Minnesota, when Seattle was playing there. Raul Ibanez was batting for the Mariners, and I was working first base. He hit a shot to right field that was a rocket, bouncing to the right fielder, Matt Lawton, on one hop. I watched the ball and then realized Lawton was going to try to throw Ibanez out at first. That's how hard the ball was hit.

In that situation umpires are trained to follow the flight of the ball, and that's what I did. I was right on the line, several steps behind first base. As I pivoted to watch the ball go toward first, I realized Ibanez was running as hard as he could right down the line, directly toward me.

I tried to get out of the way, but we collided. He absolutely smoked me. I must have been knocked in the air, because I hit the ground with a thud. I felt like a fighter who had just been knocked out. I was at a count of about seven when I finally shook some of the cobwebs out of my head and tried to prop myself up on my elbows. When I looked down, there was blood everywhere. I really thought all of my teeth had been knocked out. Ibanez was also down on the ground, and the trainers were trying to attend to us both.

After a few minutes I realized all of the blood had come from my nose, and my teeth were OK. They carried Ibanez off the field and then helped me off and made me go lie down on a table in the trainer's room in the Twins' clubhouse. They were worried I might have suffered a concussion.

I was a little bit uncomfortable lying in the Twins' training room, but I put my hat over my face and pretended to be asleep. Pretty soon I heard Tom Kelly come into the locker room screaming and yelling about the umpires, and I realized he had been ejected for one of the few times in his career. Dale Scott had kicked him out of the game, and I didn't feel like arguing with him and having him start yelling at me too. I got out of there before the game was over.

I felt good enough to fly home, but I had not had a chance to tell Sharon what had happened. She picked me up at the airport, and the first thing she said was, "What happened to you?" My face was all scraped and bruised from when I hit the AstroTurf, but I didn't know that. It looked like I had been in a fight. I told her I had gotten into a brawl with Rocky Roe, one of my partners and a good friend.

"You're kidding me," she said. Sharon loved Rocky and so did I. I said, "No, things like that happen. You ought to see him."

When I told Rocky the story later he said, "That's what you would have looked like had I gotten hold of you."

Problems for umpires don't always occur on the field or even during the course of a game. It turned out I caused a major problem for a police officer, Sgt. John Haradon, in Anaheim, by trying to be a nice guy, and I didn't even know about it for a couple of months.

If we had a 1:00 P.M. game in Anaheim, I could catch a flight back to St. Louis at 5:30 P.M. I always tried to make that flight, but it usually meant I had to get a ride with the officer to the Orange County airport. One time I told him I needed his address because I wanted to send him something for always helping me out. He didn't want anything, but he said it would be OK if I sent something to his son.

About a week later, I got a box together that included a baseball signed by Nolan Ryan and another souvenir. My off-season job then was working for Conference USA, and I occasionally had to send out packages to the referees, so I had some preprinted postage labels with a Chicago postmark, where the office was located.

I put the baseballs in a box, used the postage label with the Chicago postmark, and put my address, but no name, on the package as the return address. I didn't think anything more about it.

The next time I saw him, a couple of months later, he said, "Dave, you won't believe what happened. You caused me a major problem." It turned out when the package arrived, they called out the bomb squad to make sure it wasn't a bomb. They were concerned because it had a Chicago postmark and a Missouri address, and the officer said he didn't know anybody at that address. They had opened the package by remote control, and then sat there as the two baseballs rolled out of the package.

Two really terrible incidents involving umpires occurred during my career, one on the field and one off the field.

Probably the most despicable thing that ever happened to an umpire during my career was when Roberto Alomar of the Orioles spit on John Hirschbeck because he disagreed with Hirschbeck's call. To disagree with a call is one thing, but to spit in somebody's face is another. Alomar has been a very good player for a long time, but on this day he displayed very poor judgment.

I also was very upset with the players association and their attempts to defend Alomar and say it wasn't a big deal. It was a big deal. Alomar got suspended, but he should have had to serve the suspension during the playoffs and not get to delay it until the start of the next season.

The other terrible incident was when my good friend and longtime partner Steve Palermo was shot outside a restaurant in Dallas. It had nothing to do with him being an umpire, and certainly was a much more serious situation than the Alomar run-in. I was home on vacation when it happened, which was after we had been assigned to different crews. I always kidded Steve that he was nocturnal. He could stay up all night and still be running at 100 miles an hour the next day. I couldn't do it. He always wanted me to go out with him, and I said only on the condition that I could have my own car and leave when I wanted to. Unless it was New Year's Eve, I wouldn't stay up past 2:00 A.M.

On that night he just happened to be in the wrong place at the wrong time, and he was shot. He was paralyzed and has gone through a lot of hard work and physical rehabilitation to regain some of the use of his legs, but unfortunately he has never been able to umpire again.

Fortunately, there are far more lighthearted moments in the game than serious incidents such as those. I have been lucky enough to be involved in a good many of those over the years.

11

Intimate Conversations

The player an umpire interacts with the most on the field is the catcher. Every catcher has his own style and peculiar characteristics, and umpires quickly learn which catchers they want to work behind and which will make their jobs more difficult.

Some catchers develop great reputations, and win Gold Gloves, when many of the umpires don't think very highly of their ability. Others truly are great. I have had the privilege of working with some of the great ones. The best catcher I have seen is Ivan Rodriguez, who helped the Florida Marlins win the 2003 World Series. I honestly believe he is a better catcher than Johnny Bench, the standard by which every other catcher is measured.

Different catchers stand out for different reasons. Carlton Fisk, Bob Boone, Jim Sandberg, Terry Steinbach, and Ray Fosse are some of the more memorable catchers I worked with. One who definitely stood out during his career was Thurman Munson of the Yankees. He talked more than any catcher I ever worked behind. It didn't matter who was hitting, it didn't matter what team the Yankees were playing, it didn't matter whether the game was at home or on the road, it didn't matter who the umpire was—you could not keep Munson from talking. I heard the same thing was true about Yogi Berra.

I first got to know Munson when he was in the minors, in Syracuse, and he was the same way then. He was an excellent hitter who could hit to all fields, and he was a very popular player, but in reality he was an average catcher. He was, however, a first-class talker.

He would talk about fishing. He would ask what the hitter did on his day off. If he knew the hitter's wife, he would ask how she was doing or what the kids had been up to. He talked about movies, golf—you name it. Thurman could talk about anything. It was continuous; it didn't stop. The pitcher would be in his windup, or the ball would be on its way to the plate, and Munson would still be talking.

I know it had to unnerve a lot of hitters, and one who finally said something to Munson about it when I was behind the plate was George Brett of the Royals. During his previous at-bat, Munson had asked him about the fishing in Kansas City, about his golf game, and about the famous Kansas City barbecue. The next time Brett came up to bat, he was doing the talking.

"Listen, I want you to know," he said to Munson, "the barbecue was great, I went fishing over the All-Star break, I love to play golf, and goddamn it, I would like to hit without you talking to me." We all laughed, but it didn't stop Munson. He just started talking and didn't stop. I can see where it would affect a batter's concentration. Maybe that was what Thurman was trying to do. I didn't particularly care for it either, as I was trying to concentrate and do my job, but I had to learn to live with it.

That was just Thurman's personality. He was the captain of the Yankees and was one of the first players the Yankees began to build around when they made their transition from being a bad team in the early seventies to a great team in the last part of the decade. It was a very sad day in 1979 when Munson was killed when the plane he was piloting crashed in Ohio. He was only 32 years old.

Another catcher who lasted a long time in the game, and later was a manager, was Bob Boone. He didn't talk—he mumbled. He wore that big bar mask, and I never could understand him. He was a good guy and a good catcher, but I could never understand a word he said. Whatever he said, I said yes to. He could have said, "You missed that pitch," and I would have said yes because I couldn't understand what he said. It was just mumble, mumble, mumble.

In my early years, whenever we were working a Tigers game I hoped that Tom Haller would be catching. That's not meant as criticism of the Detroit regular, Bill Freehan; it's just testimony to how much I thought of Tom Haller. And as much as I liked Tom, his brother Bill was a great friend and mentor to me, and I always treasured his friendship.

Working with Bill Haller really helped my career. I had two miserable years working under Larry Napp and Nestor Chylak, and I have often wondered how long I would have remained an umpire if I had not been lucky enough to work with Haller in 1973. It was an added bonus that Ron Luciano was on the crew as well. Umpiring became fun again.

When we were in Cleveland the first time that year, none of us could remember the name of our dressing room attendant. When he was out of the room, Haller told me to ask his name the next time he came in the room. I did, apologizing and saying I couldn't believe I had forgotten his name.

He didn't seem offended, and he told me his name was Bill. Sheridan, Haller, and Luciano acted totally shocked and incensed that I had forgotten his name. "You dumb SOB," Haller said. "I can't believe you didn't remember Bill's name." Then Luciano piped in. "I am embarrassed he had to ask you your name, Bill," he said. Hell, neither of them knew his name either, but that was their way of having fun with the rookie crew member.

Haller was very unselfish. He would go out of his way to help a friend or to tell somebody something nice about you, something neither Napp nor Chylak believed in doing. My generation of crew chiefs learned from those older umpires, and we became determined not to follow in their path. Men like Bill Haller and Marty Springstead were ahead of me, and they helped bridge the gap between the old dominating, negative style of umpiring to one which was more compassionate and more positive. Larry Barnett, Don Denkinger, and others followed, stressing confidence rather than competitiveness, and I think that made umpiring better—and as a result made the game better.

I'll never forget the first playoff series I worked, the 1974 A.L. Championship Series between the Orioles and Oakland (with my buddy, Earl Weaver). I had the plate for the fourth game, and it turned out to be the last game, as Oakland won 2–1 to win the series and move on to the World Series.

Mike Cueller was pitching for Baltimore, and there were some close pitches that he wanted called strikes that I called balls. They were close, but they were definitely balls. I really appreciated it when Elrod Hendricks, the Orioles' catcher, was quoted in the newspapers the next day as saying that the pitches were close but he thought they were balls.

I found out years later that Haller, who lived in Illinois, made a special trip down to St. Louis to have lunch with Bob Broeg, the longtime sports editor of the *St. Louis Post-Dispatch*, for the specific purpose of telling him that I was a great umpire. I never would have found out about it if Broeg hadn't told me. That was the kind of thing Haller did, and he wasn't doing it for attention or notoriety. He was doing it because he was trying to be nice and was always looking to help a friend.

Haller was able to make the games fun, and that was important to me because I had forgotten that part of the game during the previous two seasons. As an umpire, it was the most fun I ever had in my life. Anybody who is successful in life, I think, picks up different characteristics from people they come into contact with. You make yourself a better person by learning from others. More than anything else, Haller instilled confidence in me. By showing that he believed in me, he made me a better umpire, and he continued to boost me with league officials, managers, writers, and anyone else he came in contact with.

Another umpire I worked with who kept the game fun was Durwood Merrill. When Durwood, Rocky Roe, Dale Scott, and I were together, we played a little game called Blue Bucks, in which whoever was working the plate that day had to predict the time of the game. If you got the time within five minutes either early or late, the other umpires had to pay double. If you missed it by more than five minutes, then you had to pay. If you forgot to make your prediction before the game, it cost you $5. Everything was $5. Durwood always forgot. Whoever was working at second base was the official timekeeper, and it happened frequently after the first pitch that I would point to my wrist and Durwood would see me calling time and get frustrated because he had forgotten again to predict his time and owed another $5 to the pool. Dale and Rocky would be laughing their heads off, and nobody would have any idea what we were laughing about. At the end of the year we split up the money, and my share was about enough to buy a new Seeing Eye dog.

Dale invented the game and elected himself the commissioner. Any dispute was settled with a court-martial type hearing—but any time you challenged Dale, you lost. We almost impeached him, but he overruled us.

That same year, 1973, I came home for the All-Star break and then went to the airport to catch a flight for the second half of the season. Guess who I ran into at the St. Louis airport, casually leaning against a wall smoking his pipe. Billy Martin. I didn't think he knew me that well, because this was a year before we had our big run-in, but I went up to him and said hello. He asked what I was doing in St. Louis, and I explained that I lived there. He said he and Mickey Mantle had spent the All-Star break fishing near Columbia, Missouri.

"We come up here all the time in the winter to go deer hunting," Martin said. "You ought to go with us sometime. We would have a lot of fun."

I didn't respond other than to nod my head, but I was thinking to myself, "Yeah, me and Billy Martin in the woods with a deer rifle. That's gonna work."

I kind of forgot about that meeting for a couple of weeks, until the next time we had the Tigers. Martin came up to the plate to exchange the lineup cards and said to Haller, "Hey, I saw Davey in St. Louis and invited him to go hunting with us in the winter." This time I said what I had thought at the airport.

"Let's see," I said, "I'm going to let you have a rifle and then go into the woods with you. I don't think so. Do I look stupid?"

We all laughed. Martin assured me he wouldn't shoot me. I thought maybe I was getting someplace with him, but that feeling didn't last for long.

One man who definitely had a love-hate relationship with Martin was George Steinbrenner, the Yankees' owner. He would hire and fire Martin so often I think he had a permanent locker at the stadium. I really didn't know Steinbrenner that well, but he had seemed to be on our side during the strike in 1979, and all of the umpires appreciated him for that. We knew he was tough on his managers and players.

In 1982 I was working with Nick Bremigan, and the Yankees questioned a call he made during the game. I thought Nick had made the right call, and I didn't think too much about it. The next morning in the newspapers, however, Steinbrenner absolutely annihilated Nick. He just berated Nick something awful. I was really aggravated, as the crew chief, especially since I considered George somewhat of a friend of the umpires because he was very vocal on our behalf during the 1979 strike.

When we got to the stadium that day, I called up to Steinbrenner's office and asked him to come down to our dressing room. I said we would like a minute of his time. Dick Butler was in town, and Steinbrenner hated Butler, so I wanted to get George down there and have our conversation before Butler showed up. I don't know if he knew why I was calling or not, but he agreed to come down.

I was really going to lay it on the line, that what he said was not acceptable and that I was extremely disappointed in him.

"George, we've considered you our friend and the kind of guy who has been in our corner in a lot of respects in our disputes with Major League Baseball," I said. "But I was really appalled by what you said in the newspaper today. First of all, you were wrong. I saw the replay, and other people have seen the replay. It was a very close play, but contrary to what you might think, Nick got it right. I really was upset and disappointed by your comment and your attitude toward umpires because we thought you had respect for the job we do."

Steinbrenner heard me out, and then he said, "That's what I've got a big problem with. I do everything for you guys and you guys do nothing for me."

I was shocked he said that, and I came right back at him. "Are you suggesting that we cheat?" I asked.

"I didn't say that," Steinbrenner replied. "I just said I do everything for you guys and you guys do nothing for me."

Steve Palermo was also on our crew, and he immediately started telling Steinbrenner he was wrong. I knew then and there George was not a fair person. I never considered him a friend of the umpires again. We were misled by the fact that he and Richie Phillips were close, and Richie had told us Steinbrenner was one of the guys behind the scenes pushing to get us back to work during the strike. But George was not, is not, and won't ever be a friend of umpires.

Going to New York was always a memorable experience. That was certainly the case during my first trip there, in 1971. I had been looking forward to going for a long time, and then right before the trip we had the game in Washington when Larry Napp got mad at me over the foul-tip call that got Billy Martin all upset. Napp didn't know my signal for a foul tip, and he had tried to send a runner back from second to first because he thought I called a foul ball, not a foul tip.

On the same trip to Washington, Napp had taken me with him to an Italian restaurant for lunch. He knew the owner, and I thought I would get a nice plate of spaghetti and meatballs, or veal, or something that I liked. I didn't know if it would be complimentary or if we would have to pay, but I was looking forward to a good Italian meal. Napp insisted he would do the ordering for all of us.

What a mistake that was. The waiter brought out an octopus and set it on the table. Napp had ordered octopus for lunch. I didn't like it then and don't like it now. Napp said, "You'll love it." I ate it because I didn't have any choice, but that was the first time in my life I had octopus, and the last.

Napp was really pissed at me when we got to New York because of the foul-tip call, so he wasn't talking to me. Then again, he wasn't talking to anybody else either—sounds like a fun experience. He wanted to go out for dinner, so he asked the other man on our crew, Jerry Neudecker, to go with him, and Jerry said he planned to stay in his room. I didn't know what I was going to do and went down to the lobby. Napp was sitting there, and he got up and went back to the elevator. When the door opened, Neudecker was standing there. He wasn't staying in his room—he had gone up and changed clothes and was going out, just not with Napp. So now Napp was mad at all of us.

The Longines watch company had a promotion with umpires that every two years they gave the umpires a new watch, part of their agreement as the timekeeper of major league baseball. Every new umpire was supposed to get his first watch when he made his first trip to New York. It was up to his crew chief to take him over to the office to receive his watch. I was excited about it, but Napp never took me there. By the time I got back to New York again, Longines had canceled the program. I really wanted that Longines watch, because to me it was another status symbol of being a major league umpire. Even if I had to go out and buy a watch on my own, I was going to get a Longines watch. That was exactly what I did.

The other memory I have of that first trip to New York is of the dinner I had. I didn't feel like going out to dinner, so I stopped at a deli to get a sandwich. I was just going to take it up to my room and eat while watching television. There must be two thousand delis in New York, one on every corner, just like they used to have a tavern on every corner in St. Louis. I stopped in one of the delis and ordered a bologna sandwich, potato salad, and a soda. The clerk said it was $13.50.

"Oh no, I had the bologna sandwich, potato salad, and a soda," I said, thinking he was charging me for two sandwiches or something. He insisted that was the right price. That was my initial experience with sticker shock in New York. I will say the sandwich was thick enough to feed three people, but I had just spent more than one-fourth of my $40 expense money for the day on a bologna sandwich, potato salad, and a soda.

One thing about Napp was that he always wanted recognition. He wanted people to know he was the crew chief and the man in charge. That was why he didn't like it when managers or players argued with him, and why it was so easy to pull practical jokes on him. Haller was not supposed to be on our crew in 1973, but Napp was injured and was out, so the league put Bill on our crew to take his place. Napp did come back for about a month while Haller was still there, but then he had to miss the rest of the season because of injuries.

The four of us—Napp, Haller, Luciano, and me—were working the *Game of the Week* one Saturday in Chicago, and before the game one of the producers came to our dressing room to go over the details of the broadcast. For some reason Napp wasn't there, so the producer went over everything with me, Haller, and Luciano. Haller knew he could get Napp, so he got the producer to come back when Napp was there. When he came back he said hi to Haller, Luciano, and myself by name, acting like we were best friends. Then he turned to Napp and said, "Oh, you must be the new guy."

Napp exploded, just like Haller knew he would. "The new guy? I've been in the major leagues 25 years," Napp said. Haller and Luciano were rolling on the floor they were laughing so hard.

Later, they pulled the same stunt with Jack McKeon, then the rookie manager of the Royals. Haller got Jack to say hi to all of us by name, and then turn to Napp and say, "Are you the new guy?" Napp couldn't stand it when somebody didn't recognize him. I know he ended up ejecting McKeon from a game that year, and I'm sure that pregame episode was part of the reason.

Umpires generally do not like to be recognized. It's an old cliché that if a fan comes to the game and goes home without knowing who the umpires were, then they likely have done a pretty good job. One place where that could never happen is Boston.

I've always said you could have a marbles game at midnight in Boston and draw twelve thousand people. The fans in Fenway are just unbelievable in how closely they follow the game and pay attention to what is going on.

I was working with Jim Odom, and he was kind of strange in that he never liked to go out of his hotel room to eat. His room would look like a grocery store because he would stock up on cans of soup and other food like that. He had one of those electric sticks that you can put in a can and warm up the food. He wasn't spending much of his expense money that way, and he liked it because he was a very private person.

Jim liked me because I had worked with his brother Harvey in the minors. We had a Saturday day game in Boston, and I talked Jim into going out to eat with me. We were sitting in the restaurant, and I had this strange feeling that the man at the next table was staring at us.

I tried to ignore him for as long as possible, but finally I looked over at him. He said, "You're No. 21." I had no idea what he was talking about. Then he looked at Odom and said, "You're No. 18."

I asked the guy what he was talking about, and he explained. In Boston, like in a lot of other cities, the team gave the umpires numbers on the scorecard, usually in alphabetical order, so they could put the numbers on the scoreboard and the fans would know who was working which base. This was before we actually wore numbers on our shirts or jackets.

"We were at the game today and saw you there," the man said. I couldn't believe it. This guy was able to recognize us from the stands that well. It is just a crazy sports town in general, and a great baseball town in particular. Fenway Park has always been a favorite place of mine to work, and the food in Boston is the best—especially the fish chowder at Legal Seafood.

The players on the Red Sox hated Joe Mooney, the groundskeeper, and he disliked most of them. The players didn't vote him a postseason share one year, so I think he let the grass die the next year. He didn't care. He always treated the umpires great. When we needed to get to the airport quickly on getaway day, he would get a police officer to take us in his squad car. That happened all the time, but one day it was a little more eventful than usual.

The problem with driving to the airport in Boston is you have to go through the Ted Williams Tunnel, and you have traffic from several different highways merging into two lanes. We were in the squad car, with the siren going, but none of the cars in front of us could get out of the way because they were surrounded by other cars.

There was a cab sitting next to us, and as the cars in front of us began to move, he started to inch his car up as if he were going to try to get in front of us. The police officer turned on his microphone and blared, "If you move that car, I'll kill you." I know he didn't mean to say *kill*, but that's what he said. The cabbie looked stunned and leaned over and rolled down his window and said, "You kill me?" I think he got the message.

My son, Randy, used to travel with me quite a bit when he was growing up, and I always thought the highlights of his trip would be the famous players he met—Reggie Jackson, Ken Griffey Jr., Alex Rodriguez, George Brett, Cal Ripken Jr.—all of the game's stars. That wasn't always the case, however.

Randy was 12 when he went with me to Seattle in 1993. The clubhouse attendant for the Mariners, Matt Wolcott, is a great guy, and he really took care of Randy. They sat in our dressing room playing video games during the game, which happened to be a grueling, 14-inning game. When it was over, I was exhausted. When I got back to take a shower and change clothes, Randy looked up at me with a pained expression. "Is the game over?" he said. He wanted to sit there and keep playing his games.

The next day was a getaway day, and we really had to make a 5:30 flight or we would be in a world of trouble due to a day game in Minneapolis the next day. We had a police car waiting for us after the game, and Mike Reilly was with Randy and me because he had to make the flight too. Randy rode in the front seat, and the officer had the siren going and his lights flashing on our trip to the airport. We were going 80 to 90 miles an hour, weaving around the cars as people pulled over and got out of the way, thinking a major emergency was occurring, and all it was was two umpires and my son trying to make a flight.

When we got home, all Randy could talk about was that trip to the airport, not any of the games he watched or famous players he met. That ride to the airport was the high-light of his trip.

I was fortunate to travel to a lot of great cities and to spend enough time in them that I really felt I got to know the city better than some visitors. When I first came up to the majors, Joe Cronin was the president of the American League, and he had the league office in Boston. Dick Butler worked out of that office as well. When Cronin retired, they moved the A.L. office to New York. As they were packing everything up for the move, our crew happened to be in town, so I walked over to the office to stop in and visit with Dick.

He invited me to sit down, so I moved a couple of boxes out of the chair and sat down. "I want to read you a letter," he said in his slow, Southern drawl. I was still a young umpire, and I was excited about the way my career was going. But then he started to read the letter, and it was extremely negative about one umpire. My mind was reeling as to what game this could have been, when could I have done these things, who could have written this miserable let-ter, all of those types of questions. There were not enough particulars for me to determine exactly what the letter was referring to, but I was sure it was about me. I was really wishing I hadn't come over to visit Butler that day.

When he finished the letter, Butler looked at me and said, "Who do you think wrote that letter?" My insecurity had con-vinced me the letter had to be about me; otherwise, why would Dick have read it to me, but I wasn't going to say that. I think he wanted me to say, "Chuck Tanner," or somebody else's name. Then he would have asked, "What happened with Chuck Tanner?" I was smart enough to just shake my head and say, "I don't know. I have no idea."

My heart was pounding as Dick said, "I just want you to know, this letter was written in 1932." I looked at him funny and he said, "The names and faces have changed, but the message remains the same. This is the same kind of letter I get today, just like they were written more than 40 years ago."

Butler had found that letter only because they were going through the archives so that everything could be boxed up for the move to New York. His message really hit home with me, however, and I even used that story in many of the meetings I ran as a supervisor of college basketball officials over the years.

A lot of people helped educate me throughout my career, but there was at least one day when I think I taught a young manager in Chicago, Tony LaRussa, a lesson I don't think he ever forgot.

I really like Tony. He is a baseball man, from the old school in many respects. He paid his dues over the years, but I remember the time when he was managing the White Sox and I laid into him something awful.

I was working second base, and Tony was doing everything he could to extend the length of the game. There was a close play, but nothing to argue about, and I looked and saw him trotting out. As he got close enough to hear me, I said, "What the f*** are you doing out here?" It seemed to me he thought he was being paid by the hour and not for the entire season.

Before he could answer, I continued: "Tony, let me tell you something. You are always coming out here; you've delayed this game something awful. You get this guy up, you bring this guy in. We're three hours and 40 minutes into this game, and you trot out here on a play that should not be argued about."

I was on a roll now. We hadn't even talked about the play yet. LaRussa looked stunned. I was furious, and he obviously sensed my frustration with him. I guess it was because the game had lasted so long and here he was extending it even longer on a play that should not have produced an argument. I am sure I embarrassed him, but I really wasn't trying to do that. I was just fed up with all the B.S. and the time he took day after day to play the game.

He left without discussing the play, and we finally finished the game. It was the last day of the series, and as we were packing in our dressing room, there was a knock on the door. We opened it, and Tony was standing there, wanting to know if he could talk to me.

I know he wanted me to come outside so we could talk privately, but I invited him to come on in the room, so he did. I let him talk, and he said, "I try to treat you guys as professionally as I can, but you kind of embarrassed me in front of the team. I don't know if you know this, but I am the most senior manager in this league." I knew a lot of managers had gotten fired, but I really didn't know he was the most senior man left. But then again, I really didn't care either.

When he finished, I took a deep breath and began my response. "Now let me tell you something, Tony," I said. "I don't care how long you've been here. You screw around more than anybody. You come out and make every kind of move possible. I like you and I respect you, but goddamn, Tony, if you want to argue, you have every right to argue, but be fair about it. That wasn't a close play."

About the time I stopped to take a breath, Steve Palermo saw an opening and he picked up where I had left off. Before he finished, I ended up acting as peacemaker because Steve was on the attack. I truly didn't intend to attack Tony so forcefully, but it was ridiculous. I told him that if I miss a play or it's a close play, come on out and argue, but be fair.

Tony and I had many great years together in the American League, and I kind of forgot about the incident in Chicago. I worked a lot of playoffs and other big games for LaRussa when he was in Oakland, and we got along well. Tony and I have a good relationship to this day. When he became the manager of the Cardinals, I was asked to film a couple of television commercials with him. I asked him to sign a couple of baseballs that I could donate to charity, along with one that I wanted to keep for myself. On that baseball he wrote, "To Dave, the guy who taught me to be a professional." I knew what he was talking about—that day when I laid into him in Chicago. I was somewhat honored that he thought my message on that day had an impact on his career.

Even after we became good friends, while Tony was in Oakland, I still thought he changed pitchers too often (although that isn't my responsibility). I remember we would get to the eighth inning, and I would look into the dugout and start moving my arm in an underhanded motion. I was motioning that I wanted him to bring in Dennis Eckersley so we could get the three outs we needed for the game to be over. Eck was automatic in those days, 9 or 10 pitches and the inning and the game would be over.

One day I was working second base, and in between the eighth and ninth inning, the second baseman for the A's came running up to me and said, "Mr. Phillips, Tony wanted me to tell you that out of respect for you he's not going to change pitchers in the ninth inning. He wants you to look in the dugout." I thought he was kidding, but then I looked in the dugout and Tony was dead serious. He was watching me, and when I looked in at him, he raised his hand to his cap and gave me a salute. From that day until my last, every time I worked one of Tony's games we would salute each other on the first day of the series.

I will say this about Tony. There is nobody who works harder than he does, and nobody who wants to win more than he does. He is always very serious—even in spring training. It is all about winning. But he really is a good guy.

One of my other favorite managers over the years was Whitey Herzog, whom I got to know in Kansas City before he became manager of the Cardinals. He had some good teams with the Royals, but they could never seem to get past the Yankees in the playoffs to get to the World Series.

One of Kansas City's better pitchers was Dennis Leonard, but I'll never forget one atrocious start he had. I happened to be behind the plate that day, and the eight warm-up pitches he made before the first inning were the only pitches he made that the opposing batters didn't hit.

His first pitch was hit back up the middle for a single, no big deal. Leonard reset, looked in for his sign, checked the runner, and threw his second pitch, a double off the right-center-field wall. We now had runners on second and third with no outs, starting to be a concern but still no major deal.

Now he checked both runners and threw his third pitch of the game. Another double, this time to left center. Two runs scored, and now the situation was getting a little more serious. We had had three batters, Leonard had thrown three pitches, and we had two runs in, a runner on second, and still nobody out. Herzog was in the dugout motioning for a couple of pitchers to get ready quickly in the bullpen. Then he motioned for George Brett to go to the mound from third to talk to Leonard and stall to give the relievers a little more time to warm up.

Now we were ready, and here came the next pitch. Home run. We had had four pitches, four hits, and four runs. Here came Whitey to the mound. Everybody asks me what is said during those meetings on the mound, and this was one time I had to know myself. I met Herzog at the foul line and walked to the mound with him. I was waiting for some revelation or something, but nobody said a word for several seconds. Finally Herzog looked at the catcher, Darrell Porter, and said, "Darrell, what the hell is he throwing?" Porter looked back at him and said, "Hell, Skip, how the hell would I know. I haven't caught one yet."

That broke everybody up. I left, and so did Leonard as a new pitcher came in for the Royals.

Moments like that are special, because every fan in the stands or watching the game on television can tell the results of the play, but they don't hear the little comments from players or managers. Such was the case when I was working the sixth game of the 1993 World Series between the Phillies and the Toronto Blue Jays.

In that game I was working first base, which meant that if the Phillies won and forced a seventh game, I would be working the plate. I had had the pleasure of doing that before, and I can honestly say it is not a fun experience. Everything is on the line, and the pressure is incredible. If you do a good job, that is what you were supposed to do. If something controversial happens, you become the story, and you certainly don't want that to happen.

For that reason I wasn't actively rooting for Toronto to win Game 6, clinching the Series, but I knew I certainly wouldn't be upset if that happened. I was standing in right field before the start of the ninth inning, looking at the scoreboard but not really seeing it, when I heard a loud scream coming from right behind me. "F***, f***, f***." It sounded like a microphone blaring right next to my ear.

I am jumpy anyway, and the loud scream scared the hell out of me. I turned around and saw it was Lenny Dykstra, the Phillies' center fielder. "What's wrong with you?" I asked him. He looked like he was going to explode. "I can't believe they're bringing in this f****** [Mitch] Williams," he said.

Sure enough, Williams was coming out of the Phillies' bullpen, but I didn't think anything about it—until Joe Carter hit the home run that won the World Series for the Blue Jays.

I had seen Carter enough times to know that when he had two strikes, all Williams had to do to get him to strike out was throw a slider in the dirt. Instead he threw a fastball and Carter hit one of the most famous homers in World Series history. It was an incredible moment.

I didn't know as I walked off the field that I had just worked the final World Series game of my career. I might have been a little more sentimental had I known that, but I was just glad the season was over.

The Carter home run was one play that stood out during my career, but it certainly is not the only memory I had when I retired before the 2003 season. At this point in my life, however, I am not looking back on my career. I am looking ahead, toward all of the things I want to do in the future, things I wasn't able to do that much for almost 40 years. Now I'm learning how to be a retired grandpa.

12

Looking Ahead

My daughter Kim was very sincere about wanting to attend the final game I worked in the major leagues. There was some question at the end of the 2001 season if I would or could umpire again in 2002, so Sharon and Kim came to the last game of the 2001 season, when I worked the plate at Kansas City. It was a day game, and we drove back home after the game. I honestly didn't know what would happen the next spring, but I wanted to work another year.

I felt good during the winter and in spring training, even though I was continually bothered by a sore right leg. The trainers on different teams all said they thought it was a pulled hamstring in the lower part of my thigh and that it would be OK with therapy, but I had to put ice on it every day.

My Opening Day assignment was in Cincinnati, and I was told to go to the stadium early to receive treatment on my leg. We had not even reached the third inning before my leg was hurting. The trainer had to wrap it between innings. In the seventh inning, I had to run across the infield on a play, and I felt my knee collapse. I almost fell. I knew I had hurt myself, but I wasn't sure what had happened and was afraid to ask. I should have left the game, but I didn't want to leave my crew a man short. By the time the game was over I could barely walk.

The next day was a scheduled off day and I had already planned to come home, so I hobbled through the airport and onto the plane. I got home and went in for an MRI the next day. I found out I had a badly torn meniscus that required surgery. Still, after the surgery, I hoped that I would be able to return to work in six to eight weeks.

Unfortunately, that never happened. The knee kept swelling, and over the summer of 2002 I had to have the fluid drained out of it eight times. I couldn't run, I could hardly walk without a limp, and I knew there was no way I could umpire. I would have loved to have finished the season so I could have said good-bye to my many friends around the country.

I can honestly say I would not have done anything differently during my career if I had a second chance, and that's a pretty comforting thing to be able to say. I had an unbelievable career, and a lot of people helped me along the way. Baseball gave me and my family a wonderful life.

I celebrated my 60th birthday in October 2003, and I think my major goal for the rest of my life is to be a retired grandpa. I want to enjoy my family, do some traveling—in a much different fashion than living out of a suitcase for three days and hopping on an airplane to the next city for another three-game series.

I was very fortunate to spend my 32 years in the major leagues when I did. It's a different era now. I started before the players made a lot of money, before the designated hitter, before wild-card teams and interleague play, when baseball people ran baseball. It was a different game, and I think a better game. I'm glad my career took place before the September 11 terrorist attacks, which have created so much chaos with travel restrictions. All of the extra security has changed so much of our daily routines. There is no way I could have spent as much time at home in between games now as I did, because I wouldn't be certain I could get back in time for my next game.

Baseball is in a lot of trouble, in my opinion. It got a big, unexpected boost from the success of the Cubs and the Red Sox in 2003, but that might be short-lived. There are a lot of changes I would like to see made, and they are easy for me and others to say, but they will be hard to implement. Baseball desperately needs a salary cap. There is a problem with the small market–large market differences and the competitive balance of the game. There is a basic fundamental problem when 21 of the 30 major league teams begin spring training every year knowing they have no chance of winning their division and going to the playoffs. George Steinbrenner will spend whatever it takes to win, and he has that right, because it is his money, but at some point you have to get the game back to where every team has a chance to win.

There are going to continue to be problems with ticket prices and television ratings. The players make enough money, the owners make enough money—there has got to be a way for fans to be able to go watch and enjoy the games with their families at an affordable price. I can go to the nearby Whitmoor Country Club, where I am a member, and buy a large hot dog, a bag of potato chips, and a soda for $3.50. At any major league ballpark it would cost a fan $10 or more.

We've had games delayed in starting until after 10:00 P.M. in Boston because the ownership didn't want to lose the gate. Nobody thought about that young boy in the stands who might be there for the only time that summer. By the time the game started, he was sound asleep. That's wrong.

I want my grandchildren to be able to watch and enjoy baseball the way I did as a child. I want them to have the same experiences and memories of the game that I had. I would have been devastated as a young boy if Stan Musial had been traded from the Cardinals or signed with another team as a free agent. He was my idol. I am sure youngsters in Kansas City felt that way about George Brett, and I admire him for spending his entire career with the Royals, and Kirby Puckett for doing the same with the Twins. They should not be the exceptions.

The owners have created this nightmare all by themselves. The players have the right to make as much money as they can, and no player ever held a gun to an owner's head and made him sign that contract. Players play this game because they love it, and I think they would play it for a lot less money. Salaries become an ego contest—if this player is making X amount of money, and I think I am better than he is, then I need to make more money than he does. Arbitration and free agency have been disasters for baseball.

The owners have put themselves in a position where an ordinary player who would not have been good enough to play in the Texas League when I worked there in 1966 is now making $2 million to $3 million in the major leagues, and he isn't even a starter. That needs to change.

For the owners to take the ultimate step of canceling the World Series in 1994 and get absolutely nothing in return was a gigantic mistake. I like Bud Selig, and I have known him since long before he became commissioner, but I sometimes question whether or not baseball's leadership really leads. They make phone calls and check out the opinions and concerns of others and then make whatever decision they think will please the majority. That doesn't always produce the best results. The commissioner, whoever it is, should have the authority to make decisions "in the best interests of baseball," but the current owners will never let that happen. Peter Ueberroth was a leader, but he found out the owners didn't want a leader. Bart Giamatti would have been a great commissioner had he lived, and Fay Vincent told the owners things they didn't want to hear, so they fired him.

I don't want to sound overly negative, because the game has been very good to me and my family and very good to many people. But the game is faced with serious problems that must be met head-on, not ignored in hopes they will go away. Baseball's answer to every problem seems to be to expand so that they get more money to spread around, but all that does is dilute an already weak talent pool even further. Owners have let the game get so far out of hand they are now in big trouble.

I am a conservative, but I am also a traditionalist and very sentimental about the game. I love the smell of a hot dog on the grill when I walk into a stadium. Buying a scorecard for 10 cents was a thrill. I could stare at the Green Monster all day and think about all of the Hall of Famers who have played at Fenway Park. I can't walk through Monument Park at Yankee Stadium without getting a couple of chills. I grew up during an era when baseball games were not on television every night, but were on the radio. Sitting at home listening to the game with my dad was a ritual that I know was repeated not only in my house but in thousands, if not millions, of homes across the country. I could close my eyes and create a mental picture of the ballpark, even if it was in a faraway city.

When we weren't out in the park playing, we were listening to the game on the radio. However many kids were there that day, we chose up sides and played. The game was fun. We didn't need organized Little Leagues and fancy uniforms. All we needed was a bat, a ball, and the neighbor kids. In my neighborhood, everybody wanted to be Stan Musial, and he and the other Cardinals seemed larger than life to me, and I know I am not the only person who feels that way about this game and the home team.

Baseball is a game of records and statistics, and that has forever changed. Steroids, improved equipment, the watered-down talent pool that brings inferior pitchers to the major leagues, and the smaller stadiums are all reasons that make historical comparisons difficult. What makes baseball unique is that you can look back at something that happened in 1900 or 1920 and compare it to what happened in the fifties and sixties. That's when baseball started to change. You can't compare 2003 to 1920, because it is not the same game.

The designated hitter is a disgrace in my opinion. Joe Cronin put it in as an experiment in the American League in 1971 because he was worried about offense. It should be an embarrassment to the league. It is still in place as an experiment. The rule has never been changed. The players union will never give it up, because that spot on a team is almost always reserved for an older, high-salaried player.

Television has also changed the game. When I first came to the big leagues, the White Sox, Yankees, and other teams started their home games at 8:00 P.M. The games started lasting so long they couldn't get the highlights on the 10:00 P.M. news, so they moved the games up to 7:30 P.M., and then to 7:05 P.M. Yet there are still too many nights now when the games aren't over by 10:00 P.M.

ESPN shows every highlight of every game, and players try to hit home runs so they can go home and watch themselves on *Baseball Tonight.* It takes away the desire of the fans to go to the game. Nobody cares who won or lost. All that matters is who hit the farthest home run. Television highlights don't show the ground ball to second that advanced the runner to third, allowing him to score the winning run on a fly ball.

My first year in the majors, I worked a day game at Yankee Stadium, then stopped in a bar to get a sandwich when I got back downtown. The bartender recognized me and said, "You had a good game today." I asked if he had gone to the game, and he said no, he had watched it on television. I was shocked that the Yankees had televised a home game. Now, almost every game is televised whether the team is at home or on the road.

Playoff games did not sell out when I first worked in the major leagues, and many do not sell out now. That prompted baseball to start charging more for the tickets. They went into the scalping business, just like the NFL did with its playoffs and the Super Bowl. Baseball doubled the price of World Series tickets, from $75 each to $150, in one year. The networks have to pay so much money for the rights to broadcast the games that they are forced to over-charge for their commercials. That means there will never be another World Series game played during the day, and that's another giant mistake. Baseball is losing an entire generation of fans by playing those games so late that they don't end until midnight on school nights.

Kids have so many more choices of activities now than we did when I was growing up. They don't care about baseball, because they say the games are too long and too boring. It makes me sick, but it should make baseball's leadership sick.

Baseball was a great game. It can be again, but only if the people in charge decide to do something about it.

What made baseball great was the people—the great players, the colorful managers, the broadcasters, the fans. Those personalities are gone from the game, and that's what the game has lost. The game is too rigid now, too structured and too commercialized. Everybody is too worried about money.

The owners, the players, the union, and the agents need to sit down and figure out a way to get baseball back to where it used to be, before it is too late. I don't think we have reached the point where the game can't be saved, but the clock is ticking.

My income has been completely derived from sports—earned either as an umpire or by officiating college basket-ball—throughout my adult life. I feel very fortunate because a lot of people go through life and never find a job that they like or enjoy. I found not only a job I liked but also a pro-fession I truly loved.

My dad took a great deal of pride in the umpiring profession. I consider myself lucky and proud to have followed in his footsteps and to have had such a lengthy and enjoyable career. I was honored to work several World Series and numerous championship playoff series. I was selected to travel to Japan in 1981 to umpire games between the Kansas City Royals and several Japanese teams, and I conducted several clinics in Europe for the air force. I have enjoyed being able to participate in many charity functions, to serve on numerous boards of directors, and to fulfill speaking engagements around the country, all because of my association with baseball.

I have met presidents, politicians, movie stars, and entertainers. George Bush and his son George W. Bush are two of my favorites because they are great friends of baseball. When George W. owned the Rangers, he frequently stopped in our dressing room to visit, and I always enjoyed our conversations.

I was inducted into the Missouri Sports Hall of Fame in February 2004; I was the first umpire to ever receive that honor, for which I'm very grateful.

There are far too many memories and highlights to list them all, but I know I am most grateful for all of the great friends I have made over the years—again, far too many to mention.

I sincerely hope my grandchildren will be able to develop the same feelings about baseball that I had as a youngster. I know I truly enjoyed my entire career both on and off the field, and I sincerely hope umpires of the future will be able to enjoy their jobs as much as I did mine.

Index

Index